Essentials of
Political Research

Essentials of Political Science

James A. Thurber, American University, Editor

The Essentials of Political Science Series will present faculty and students with concise texts designed as primers for a given college course. Many will be 200 pages or shorter. Each will cover core concepts central to mastering the topic under study. Drawing on their teaching as well as research experiences, the authors present narrative and analytical treatments designed to fit well within the confines of a crowded course syllabus.

Essentials of American Government, David McKay

Essentials of Political Research, Alan D. Monroe

Essentials of
POLITICAL
RESEARCH

Alan D. Monroe

Illinois State University

Westview Press
A Member of the Perseus Books Group

Essentials of Political Science

Copyright © 2000 by Westview Press, A Member of the Perseus Books Group

Published in 2000 in the United States of America by Westview Press, 5500 Central Avenue, Boulder, Colorado 80301–2877, and in the United Kingdom by Westview Press, 12 Hid's Copse Road, Cumnor Hill, Oxford OX2 9JJ

Find us on the World Wide Web at www.westviewpress.com

Library of Congress Cataloging-in-Publication Data
Monroe, Alan D.
    Essentials of political research / Alan D. Monroe.
        p. cm — (Essentials of political science)
    Includes biographical references and index.
    ISBN 0-8133-6866-9 (pbk.)
    1. Political science—Research.   2. Political science—Methodology.   I. Title.
    II. Series.

JA71 .M635 2000
320'.07'2—dc21
                                                                00-039878

The paper used in this publication meets the requirements of the American National Standard for Permanence of Paper for Printed Library Materials Z39.48–1984.

10   9   8   7   6   5   4   3   2   1

For Paula, Melissa, and Mollie

Contents

Tables and Figures

Preface

This book is intended as a comprehensive text for an introductory course in research methods for the social sciences. While written with students of Political Science in mind, it would be appropriate for similar disciplines.

The intention in this book is to concentrate on the *essentials*. Given the broad scope of this book and its relatively brief length, I have attempted to concentrate on what seem to be the most important points necessary to understanding the research process. At the same time, I have attempted to cover those points in sufficient depth that the reader will be able to understand them. Therefore, it has been necessary to dispense with some technical details that a longer and more advanced text might include.

In writing this book, I have drawn on over twenty-five years of teaching this subject matter to students of Political Science at Illinois State University. Drafts of the manuscript have been used as a text for several semesters, and my students have been helpful in correcting and refining the text. Any errors that remain, however, are my responsibility.

Alan D. Monroe

1

The Scientific Study of
Research Questions

The reason we have accumulated knowledge of any subject—
whether physics, philosophy, or political science—is that others
have undertaken systematic investigations of particular topics and
reported the results. But why is it important for people who are
not professionals in those fields, particularly students, to know
about research methodology—that is, how research is done? There
are several answers to this question. First of all, students in any
subject spend most of their class time and study time learning
about the results of past research. They can better understand
what those findings mean if they have some familiarity with the
methods used to obtain them. When they go beyond textbooks
and the classroom, they may have to judge whether a piece of research is valid and whether its results ought to be believed. Second,
students are often asked to do some research on their own—the
dreaded term paper. Although they may be able to get by with just
summarizing what others have said, their papers will be more
meaningful and rewarding if they can actually conduct original investigations. In advanced courses—and certainly in graduate
school—this is a necessity.

The need to understand and to be able to use research methods
continues beyond one's formal education. In all sorts of occupations, particularly those into which students from political science
and related disciplines go, employees are asked to make decisions
about the value of research methods and findings. Consultants
often use such methods, and those contracting for their services

should be able to evaluate their reports and findings. Similarly, people may have to conduct some sort of research project on their own, such as a survey of potential clients. Understanding research methods is useful to all of us beyond the workplace as well—for example, as citizens who may be asked to vote on a tax referendum for a project recommended by a consultant's research findings. Those who become active in politics, in local government, and in citizen organizations have a particular need to know something about research methods.

This book is an introduction to the process of research. It deals only with *scientific* research, the meaning of which is discussed below. Although the book is designed for students of politics and therefore uses examples from that field and gives more attention to the techniques that political scientists use most frequently, the methods are common to all social sciences, including sociology, economics, and psychology.

What Does It Mean to Be Scientific?

There are many definitions of science. Perhaps the simplest one would be *an attempt to identify and test empirical generalizations*. The first key part here is *empirical*. The term refers to the facts, or the real world: that which exists and can be known through the experiences of our senses—what can be seen, touched, heard, and smelled. Much of what we might believe about things is not empirical, but rather *normative*—that is, it reflects our judgments about what should be. A vitally important point to understand is that scientific methods cannot deal directly with nonempirical questions; the next section of this chapter explains how to identify them.

The purpose of the methods and techniques of science is to test empirical statements. The testing must be *objective*, that is, its results must not be dependent on any particular researcher's biases. Under this requirement—which is known by its technical term, *intersubjective testability*—a finding cannot be accepted unless it can be replicated by others. For that reason, political science journals are increasingly requiring that authors of articles reporting empirical research make their data available for analysis by others. Moreover, it is always important that scientific research reports carefully explain how data were collected and analyzed.

The other key part of science is *generalization*. Scientists seek to make statements about entire classes of objects, not just individual cases, though the observation must be of individuals. The facts that Mr. Smith has only a grade school education and does not vote, whereas Ms. Jones has an advanced degree and always votes, are of little value by themselves. But when we collect that information on a large number of people from many places and across time, we can make a generalization that people with more education are more likely to vote than people with less education.

The main purpose of science is to *explain and predict*, and scientific explanation requires generalizations. Consider this simple logical syllogism:

1. If there is a high rate of economic growth, the incumbent president is usually reelected. (Generalization)
2. There was a high rate of growth in 1996. (Observation)
3. Therefore, President Clinton, the incumbent, was reelected in 1996.

This argument is an explanation, though not the only one, for the election outcome. Note that the same reason could also be a basis for a *prediction* of who would win the election, assuming that the economic data were available beforehand. The point is that we must have generalizations to explain what has happened and to predict what will happen—and indeed, to understand how the world works. If we have generalizations about many phenomena, we can put them together into *theories*, a term defined in the next chapter.

The election example illustrates another important point. The generalizations made in the social sciences are almost never absolute. Some presidents running in good economic times are defeated. Some people with high levels education do not vote, and some with little schooling vote regularly. Although generalizations may not state this probabilistic quality explicitly, it is almost always implied.

Distinguishing Empirical and Normative Questions

As noted earlier, science can answer only empirical questions or test empirical statements. Therefore, it is important to be able to distinguish empirical statements from other kinds, particularly when one is selecting a topic for scientific research.

Empirical statements refer to what is or is not true and can be confirmed or disproved by sense experience. Whether they are simple descriptive statements ("Bill Clinton was reelected in 1996") or deal with complex relationships ("Controlling for presidential popularity, the greater the increase in average real income, the higher the proportion of votes received by the incumbent party"), they are empirical if objective analysis of data from sensory observation could potentially prove or disprove them. It does not matter whether they are posed as questions or as statements or if they deal with the past, present, or future ("Will the Democrats win the next election?").

Normative questions are different. They deal with value judgments, that is, questions of what is good or bad, desirable or undesirable, beautiful or ugly. Examples could include: "Was Bill Clinton a good president?" "Should taxes be increased?" "Is democracy the best form of government?" According to the philosophy of science, these normative questions are fundamentally different because they cannot be answered objectively. The answers to normative questions depend on the value judgments of the individual who answers them. Even if we find a normative proposition with which virtually everyone agrees ("Murder is bad"), it still is normative and not empirically testable.

There is one other classification of questions and statements: *analytical*. Analytical statements refer to propositions whose validity is completely dependent on a set of assumptions or definitions rather than on empirical observation. Mathematics, including classical geometry with its proofs from postulates, is an example of purely analytical reasoning familiar to most people. Social scientists, particularly economists, sometimes deal with analytical questions as a way of investigating the way things would be if abstract theories were true. This activity can help to develop empirical propositions whose testing would shed some light on the applicability of theories. Political scientists have often looked at different methods of casting and counting votes to see what the consequences would be under these arrangements.

Box 1.1 presents some examples and comments on the rationale for their classification. Exercise A at the end of the chapter presents some additional examples for readers to test their understanding.

BOX 1.1   Empirical, Normative, and Analytical Sentences

1. "Sixty-two percent of the American people think the president is doing a good job." (Empirical) Although the evaluation is obviously normative, the statement is an empirical one about what value judgments people make, and it can be empirically tested by surveys.

2. "Most African Americans vote Republican." (Empirical) As it happens, this is a false empirical statement, but it is still empirical and could tested by observation.

3. "Abortion is a fundamental right guaranteed by the U.S. Constitution." (Normative) The Supreme Court has in fact taken this position, but it is still a normative judgment.

4. "Is it more important to adopt policies that will protect the environment or policies that will maximize economic growth?" (Normative) Although the word "important" is not necessarily normative, it is used as a value judgment here, as the question really asks which policy goal is more desirable.

5. "Is it possible for a candidate to be elected president by the electoral college without having the greatest number of popular votes?" (Analytical) This question asks whether it is possible, so it can be answered simply by looking at the way the electoral system is set up and constructing a hypothetical scenario about how it could happen. (It actually has happened several times, but that is not the point.)

6. "It is better to have nonpartisan elections for local government, because then there would be less corruption." (Normative) Although the extent of corruption under a nonpartisan system might be an empirical question, the judgment that nonpartisanship is therefore better is normative.

continues

> *continued*
>
> 7. "A democratic political system is one in which government tends to respond to the wishes of the citizens." (Analytical) This is simply a definition and does not require any empirical observation to test it.

Reformulating Normative Questions as Empirical

On learning that scientific study does not attempt to answer normative questions, one might well object that this excludes many of the most interesting and important topics, especially in politics. Indeed, this was the basis of much of the objection to the scientific orientation that became dominant in political science in the 1950s and 1960s. After all, the political process is largely concerned with questions about what ought to be.

In fact scientific research can deal with normative phenomena, but it can do so only indirectly as it seeks to answer empirical questions. This can be done by taking the normative questions that motivate our interest and reformulating them as empirical questions in one of two ways. The first method, which is the easiest, though often not the most valuable, is to change the frame of reference. This means moving from a normative judgment to a question about the normative judgments some person or persons make. We have already seen an example of this in Box 1.1. Although the question of whether the president is doing a good job or not is a normative one, the question of whether the public thinks his performance is good is an empirical one. Such reformulations can be made with any set of individuals—the public, political scientists, or left-handed civil servants.

Although changing the frame of reference may be quite useful for some topics, such as presidential approval ratings, for others the results produced would be trivial. The other method of reformulating normative into empirical questions is to ask empirical questions about the assumptions behind normative judgments.

Most normative judgments are based in part on beliefs about what is empirically true. For instance, many people believe that democracy is a better form of government than dictatorship because they believe that democracies are more stable, are less likely to start wars, and produce greater economic development. But are

BOX 1.2　Reformulating Normative Sentences as
Empirical by the Frame of Reference and Empirical
Assumptions Methods

1. Should term limits be adopted for Congress? (Normative)
Do most political scientists favor term limits? (Frame) Would
term limits increase the influence of interest groups on congressional decisionmaking? (Assumptions)

2. Would it be a good idea to legalize drugs? (Normative)
Do most Americans favor legalization of drugs? (Frame)
Would legalization of drugs decrease the occurrence of other
crimes? (Assumptions) How much would legalization of
drugs increase the frequency of addiction? (Assumptions)

3. The United States should continue to send troops to the
third world to attempt to restore order. (Normative) Nations
in the European Union favor the U.S. sending of troops in
most cases. (Frame) The support of peacekeeping activities
with U.S. troops generally has not resulted in long-term prevention of disorder in the past. (Assumptions)

4. Strict limits on campaign spending for congressional
elections should be adopted. (Normative) Democrats favor
spending limits more than do Republicans. (Frame) Spending limits tend to increase the reelection rate for incumbents.
(Assumptions)

these assumptions correct? Scientific investigation may be able to
test them. Similarly, most recommendations for public policy
changes are based on assumptions about what the effects of those
decisions will be. Advocates of a tax decrease may argue that it will
stimulate the economy, thereby creating jobs and ultimately increasing tax revenue. Whether or not these effects would occur is
an empirical question that economists attempt to answer. Box 1.2
presents some examples of reformulation using both methods, and
Exercise B at the end of the chapter offers more.

The assumptions method can be valuable in formulating interesting and important research questions, but its limitations must be kept in mind. Although empirical reformulation may lead to research that will aid normative decisionmaking, empirical research can never actually answer a normative question. To use the previous examples, a believer in democracy might favor that form of government even if it were not more stable, peaceful, or prosperous, and persons with particular economic interests may favor or oppose a tax cut regardless of its overall effect on the economy.

Research Questions

Scientific research, like any other serious intellectual investigation, begins with a question that the research is intended to answer. Since this starting point will determine the design and conduct of the inquiry, the formulation of a research question (also called a research problem) is of paramount importance. It is not only professional scientists who must articulate a research question, but also beginners. How often do students start with term paper topics—but not research questions—and assemble stacks of information and write extensive summaries, only to have instructors criticize the resulting papers for lack of focus? A thoughtfully chosen and clearly established research question can avoid this problem in both scientific and nonscientific inquiry.

But what are the elements of a desirable research question? This is difficult to answer in the abstract, but several criteria should be kept in mind in choosing a topic and formulating a scientific research question. The first criterion is *clarity*. Aside from simply being comprehensible in the usual sense, this means that a question must be specific enough to give direction to the research, and general enough that it suggests what a possible answer would be. For instance, the question "Why is voter turnout low in the United States?" gives no direction as to whether we should look at citizen attitudes, election laws, or any number of other possible factors. A more useful version would be "Is voter turnout reduced by political alienation?" or, even better, "Does the use of election day voter registration increase turnout?" Similarly, a question such as "How can poverty in less-developed nations be remedied?" would be improved by asking, "Does foreign investment result in long-term increases in the standard of living?"

Although research questions require specificity for clarity, limiting their scope in time or place is neither necessary nor generally desirable. To restrict the above examples to particular cities or elections in the case of voter turnout, or a single nation in the case of economic development, would reduce the theoretical significance and practical relevance of the findings (these two criteria are discussed below). Although a given research project may well be confined to a single time or place as a practical matter, it is the more general question that science seeks to answer.

The second criterion is *testability*, and it is an absolute requirement. The research question must be one that can be potentially answered by empirical inquiry. First of all, it must be an empirical question, not a normative question; two methods for reformulating a normative question as an empirical one have already been presented. A second consideration is whether the necessary investigation can be devised and carried out with the resources available. Researching questions about attitudes of voters in presidential elections may require conducting national surveys, which is a costly enterprise beyond the budget of even professional political scientists. But those who lack this ability, including undergraduate students, may still pursue such questions by making use of surveys conducted by others or by conducting surveys of limited populations.

Another criterion is *theoretical significance*. Answering the question should potentially increase our general knowledge and understanding of the topic. Evaluating a potential research question therefore requires finding out what past research findings exist or, at least, what others have generally assumed to be true. Although political scientists may not have conducted much theorizing on a given subject, researchers in other fields may have developed theories that can be applied. Working from existing theories or past research does not mean that the investigator necessarily believes them to be correct. Indeed, the suspicion that existing explanations are fundamentally inaccurate or no longer applicable in a changing world is often a major motivation for research. But whether the research proves the past suppositions to be right or wrong, its significance would greater than if the question came only from the researcher's imagination, because it represents building on previous research.

A similar criterion is *practical relevance*. Answering the research question should be useful in some real-life application. This is particularly true for questions dealing with causes of social problems and their possible solutions ("Have time limits on eligibility for welfare payments increased employment rates among past recipients?"). Although there is a common tendency to think of theoretical significance and practical relevance as opposing qualities, the strongest research questions have some of both. The point is that there should be some potential value in answering a research question—either it should increase our general knowledge of the world, or it should help in accomplishing something someone wants to do. If neither is true, then why pursue that topic?

A final criterion is *originality*. This does not mean that a research question must be completely new, but it does mean that the answer should not be so well established that there is little reason to expect a different outcome. For example, the generalization that people with more education have a higher voter turnout rate than people with less education is so well established—in the United States and in the world in general—that pursuing it as a research topic would not be a wise use of resources, even for an undergraduate student. However, there may well be related questions—such as why contemporary college students have low rates of political participation, or conditions under which members of ethnic minorities with limited education become activists—that would be more promising.

Thus there are five criteria to keep in mind in selecting a question for scientific research. It should be *clear* and reasonably specific. It must be empirical to be *testable*, and it must be a question that can be investigated given available resources. It should have some degree of either *theoretical significance* or *practical relevance*, and preferably both. Finally, it should have some degree of *originality*. Box 1.3 presents several examples of possible research questions, their strengths and weaknesses, and ways in which they might be strengthened. Exercise C at the end of the chapter does the same.

The Scientific Research Process

Figure 1.1 presents an outline of the entire research process, each stage of which will be covered in this book. As discussed earlier, we must always start with a survey of past research and theorizing on a topic. Then one or more research questions that meet the five criteria can be formulated. From there, keeping in mind what was already known, hypotheses are developed (Chapter 2). Then we prepare a research design that could test those hypotheses (Chapter 3).

BOX 1.3   Evaluating and Improving
Research Questions

1. Question: "How has American politics changed since the 1994 elections?" This question is extremely vague, and so it does not meet the criterion of clarity. If it were improved in specificity—for example, "Has congressional voting been more along party lines since 1994?"—then it would be much clearer and readily testable. Moreover, it would have some degree of significance, since the extent of party regularity in legislatures is a variable that political scientists have long studied, and it would have practical relevance for those who seek to influence public policy.

2. Question: "Should the United States give military aid to Bolivia next year?" This question is obviously normative and therefore not testable. Additionally, it deals with only a single case, and therefore would be low in significance. It could be transformed by using the assumptions method and further strengthened by posing it more generally. Improved: "Does receiving military aid cause less-developed nations to increase or decrease their spending on health and education?"

3. Question: "Do the spouses of U.S. senators tend to have higher levels of education than the spouses of U.S. representatives?" This question is clear, easily testable, and probably original. However, it is completely lacking in any theoretical significance or practical relevance.

Next, we collect the necessary data (Chapters 4 and 5). Since empirical researchers in the social sciences typically collect large amounts of information, statistical analysis usually is needed to evaluate it (Chapters 6, 8, 9, and 10). Finally, we draw our conclusions and present them in a research report (information on presenting findings graphically appears in Chapter 7). These findings then add to the body of existing knowledge and may lead us or others to raise new research questions.

FIGURE 1.1 Stages in the research process

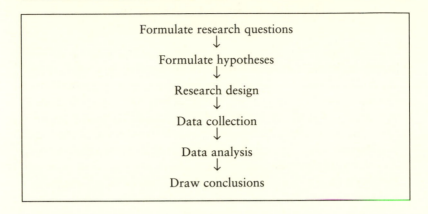

Exercises

Suggested answers to these exercises appear at the end. It is strongly suggested that the reader attempt to complete the exercises before looking at the answers. Note that on Exercises B and C the answers provided are only suggestions, as the problems could be answered well in a number of ways.

Exercise A

Identify each of the following as empirical, normative, or analytical.

1. If a foreign policy decision would increase U.S. exports, then that's what should be done.
2. Putting courtroom trials on television distorts the judicial process and defeats justice.
3. Why do communist and socialist nations have lower incomes than capitalist nations?
4. Allowing people to carry concealed weapons lowers the crime rate.
5. If guns are outlawed, only outlaws will have guns.
6. The current practice of campaign fund-raising is corrupting the character of American democracy.
7. People who think that politicians are dishonest are less likely to vote than those who trust government.
8. Is affirmative action an unconstitutional form of reverse discrimination?

9. Political parties have fulfilled a majority of their platform promises over the years.
10. Is political instability related to political change?

Exercise B

Each of the following sentences is normative. Reformulate them using the empirical assumptions method.

1. Should the United States increase the amount of foreign aid it gives to poor nations?
2. Would we be better off if Congress and the presidency were controlled by the same political party?
3. Since poor education is the biggest problem facing the nation, spending for schools should be increased.
4. Negative campaign advertising is what's wrong with elections today.
5. Do we need a new political party in this country to represent middle-of-the-road views?

Exercise C

Following are some potential research questions. Evaluate each on the criteria of clarity, testability, theoretical significance, practical relevance, and originality. If there are serious weaknesses, suggest an improved version.

1. How democratic is the U.S. political system?
2. Who shot President Kennedy?
3. Do appointed judges make fairer decisions than elected judges do?
4. Which member of the U.S. House had the poorest attendance record on roll call voting in the last session?
5. Are voters' decisions in recent presidential elections influenced more by their attitudes on abortion or by their perceptions of the economic situation?

Suggested Answers to Exercises

Exercise A

1. Normative
2. Normative

3. Empirical
4. Empirical
5. Analytical
6. Normative
7. Empirical
8. Normative
9. Empirical
10. Analytical

Exercise B

1. Is the amount of U.S. economic aid received by a nation related to subsequent growth in per capita income?
2. Are federal budget deficits greater in years of unified party control than in years of divided control?
3. Do students in school districts that spend more on public education have higher test scores after the average education and income of parents in those districts are taken into account?
4. Was the frequency of negative advertising greater in the 1990s than in the 1980s?
5. Would a new political party with an ideologically centrist position on most issues receive more than 20 percent of the votes?

Exercise C

1. The problem here is a lack of clarity, as the term *democracy* is used in many ways and each has many aspects. If made more specific, the question certainly could have considerable theoretical significance and/or practical relevance, for example, "How much of the time are the policy decisions of the U.S. government in agreement with the preferences of a majority of the people?"
2. The question is clear and specific, and its answer could conceivably have some practical relevance. But it is not likely to be testable, and it is definitively unoriginal. In addition, it lacks theoretical significance, as it deals with only a single event. Improved: "Do political assassinations in modern democracies lead to changes in the governing political party?"
3. The problem here is that fairness is a normative concept, so the question not testable. If some empirical measure were

substituted, then the question could be testable, significant, and relevant, for example, "Are elected judges more likely than appointed judges to render verdicts favoring the defendant in criminal cases?"

4. This is a clear question that could easily be tested, but it lacks any theoretical significance and has little practical relevance. Improved: "Does a representative's attendance record affect his or her chances of reelection?"

5. This is a reasonably clear and testable question that has considerable theoretical significance for our knowledge of voting behavior and some practical relevance for contemporary politics. Although it is not completely original, the question is still of interest, as the answer is not completely clear and it needs to be reinvestigated for each new election. Therefore, no improvement is needed.

2

Building Blocks of the Research Process

This chapter presents a number of different concepts involved in the research process. The goal here is not to teach terminology but to help you keep these ideas straight as you work with them. The concepts discussed in this chapter constitute the very heart of social science research, and familiarity with them is not only helpful in understanding how others conduct research but also vital to being able to do it yourself. Although these concepts might seem very abstract at first, by the end of the chapter you should be able to apply some of them to specific examples yourself.

Theories, Hypotheses, and Operational Definitions: An Overview

One of the difficulties in simply describing these building blocks of research is that science operates at several levels. Box 2.1 contains a diagram of these levels with two examples. Science starts and ends with *theories*. Although the term *theory* is used in wide variety of ways, it could be defined as *a set of empirical generalizations about a topic*. A theory consists of very general statements about how some phenomenon, such as voting decisions, economic developments, or outbreaks of war, occurs. But theories are too general to test directly because they make statements about the relationship between abstract concepts—such as economic development and political alienation—

BOX 2.1   An Overview of the Levels of Research

LEVEL
THEORY: Concept 1 is related to Concept 2.
HYPOTHESES: Variable 1 is related to Variable 2.
OPERATIONAL: Operational Definition 1 is related to
           Operational Definition 2.

EXAMPLE 1:
THEORY: Economic development is related to political
           development.
HYPOTHESES: The more industrialized a nation, the
           greater the level of mass political participation.
OPERATIONAL: The higher the percentage of the labor
           force engaged in manufacturing, according to the
           United Nations Yearbook, the higher the
           percentage of the population of voting age that
           participated in the most recent national election,
           according the *Statesman's Yearbook*.

EXAMPLE 2:
THEORY: Socioeconomic status affects political participation.
HYPOTHESES: The higher a person's income, the more
           likely he or she is to vote.
OPERATIONAL: The higher a survey respondent's answer
           when he or she is asked, "What is your house-
           hold's annual income," the more likely that
           person will answer "Yes" when asked, "Did you
           vote in the election last November?"

---

that are complex and not directly observable. To actually investigate the empirical applicability of a theory, it must be brought down to more specific terms.

This is done by testing *hypotheses*. A hypothesis is simply *an empirical statement derived from a theory*. The logic linking the two is that if a general theory is correct, then the more specific hypothesis derived from it ought to be true. Moreover, if the hypothesis is confirmed by empirical observation, then our confidence in the general theory is increased. However, if a hypothesis is not confirmed, we must question the validity of the theory from which it was derived. Hypotheses are also related to our research questions, which were discussed in the previous chapter. Hypotheses are those answers to our research questions that seem to be the most promising on the basis of theory and past research.

Hypotheses are statements about *variables*. A variable is *an empirical property that can take on two or more different values*. As the examples in Box 2.1 illustrate, hypotheses are much more specific than theoretical statements. But even variables are not specific enough for observation. Each variable in a hypothesis must have an *operational definition*, that is, *a set of directions as to how the variable is to be observed and measured*. Constructing operational definitions is a vital part of the research process and is discussed later in this chapter.

The stages illustrated in Box 2.1 show how we move from very general theoretical propositions down to specific instructions about how to measure variables, whether by looking on a particular column in a reference book or asking a specific question in a survey.

Types of Hypotheses

Hypotheses make statements about variables. These statements can take a variety of forms, as shown in Figure 2.1. If the hypothesis makes a statement about only one property or variable, then it is referred to as a *univariate hypothesis*. A *multivariate hypothesis* makes a statement about how two or more variables are related.

Most scientific hypotheses are multivariate as well as *directional*, that is, they specify not just that the variables are related to one another but also what the direction of the relationship is. In a *positive* or *direct* relationship between two variables, as one variable rises, the other tends to rise; for example, "The more education one has, the greater one's income." In *negative* or *inverse* relationships, the opposite occurs, that is, as one variable rises, the other tends to fall; for example, "The wealthier a nation, the lower its level of illiteracy." In *nominal* relationships, the hypothesis does predict the direction, but one or both of the variables are

FIGURE 2.1 Types of hypotheses and examples

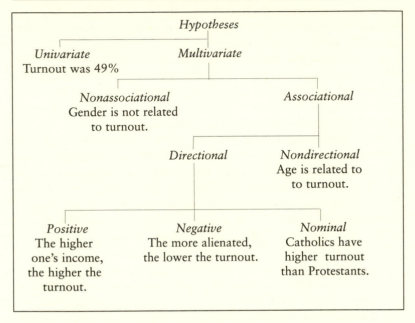

such that they cannot be described in quantitative terms. An example of such a nominal relationship would be "Catholics are more likely than Protestants to vote Republican."

Theoretical Role

In most multivariate hypotheses, each variable takes on a particular *theoretical role*; the presumed causal relationship between the variables is specified. Causality is discussed in greater detail in Chapter 3, but here an introduction to the concept is needed.

Independent variables are those presumed in the theory underlying the hypothesis to be the *cause* and *dependent variables* are the *effects* or consequences. Although this distinction is sometimes difficult to make, in most hypotheses it is apparent. The statement may include explicit language to that effect—for example, "causes," "leads to," or "results in." In other instances, the substantive nature of the variables permits only one direction. For instance, if we hypothesize a relationship between a person's gender and his or her attitudes, it is conceivable only that gender is the independent variable and attitude is the dependent variable. (Which gender you are might influence your thoughts, but it is not possible for your thoughts to affect your gender.)

Often the nature of the relationship lies in the timing between variables. Gender and race, for example, are determined before birth. As a practical matter, most social characteristics of individuals, such as education, religion, and region of residence, are usually determined early in life. In contrast, aspects of political behavior, such as voting decisions and opinions, are subject to alteration with the passage of time. Hence we usually presume that the social factors are independent variables and the behaviors are dependent variables. Similarly, if we hypothesize a relationship between demographic attributes (economic development, urbanization, and the like) of geographic or political units (e.g., nations, states, or cities) on the one hand, and their behaviors (e.g., policies they adopt) on the other, then the demographics would probably be the independent variables. Ultimately the decision as to which are the independent and which the dependent variables is based on our theoretical understanding of the phenomena in question.

The *control variable* takes on a third theoretical role. Control variables are *additional variables that might affect the relationship between the independent and dependent variables.* When control variables are used, the intent is to ensure that their effects are excluded—that is, to ensure that it is not these variables that are in fact responsible for the variations observed in the dependent variable. Control variables in a hypothesis are always explicitly labeled as such, usually with the terms *controlling for* or *holding constant.*

Control variables can go a long way toward clarifying relationships between variables. It can be all too easy, when we find that two variables are related and we look no further, to conclude that one caused the other. But we must always be alert to the possibility that other factors may be involved. To take a well-known example, African Americans have lower rates of voter turnout than do whites. One might readily conclude that race is somehow the cause of lower turnout and advance explanations based on racial discrimination in voter registration or cultural differences in political attitudes. Yet, as a number of studies have shown, if we statistically control for other characteristics such as education, economic status, and region of residence, the difference largely or even entirely disappears. In other words, if we compare African Americans and whites who have the same level of education and income and live

in the same part of the country, each is as likely as the other to vote
(Wolfinger and Rosenstone, 1980, 90–91). This would lead us to
conclude that the main reasons for racial disparity in voter turnout
are these demographic factors; certainly, any investigation of
turnout should control for them.

Box 2.2 presents several examples of hypotheses, identifying the
variables and their roles. Note that although most multivariate hypotheses have only one independent and one dependent variable, it
is possible to have more than one of each. Box 2.2 also identifies
the *unit of analysis* implied in the hypothesis, a concept discussed
in the next section. Exercise A provides additional examples.

Units of Analysis

As mentioned earlier, variables are empirical properties, but of
what are they properties? The answer is the unit of analysis in the
hypothesis, that is, *the objects that the hypothesis describes*. In
many hypotheses the unit of analysis is explicit. If we say that
people with one characteristic also tend to have another characteristic, then the unit is the individual person. If the hypothesis says
that some types of nations are higher in some factor than others,
then nations are the unit of analysis.

Sometimes the unit of analysis in a hypothesis is not so obvious.
Indeed, there may be a choice. If the hypothesis is simply that "income is related to voter turnout," the unit of analysis could be individuals, or it could be groups of people, such as the populations
of states or cities, for both individuals and groups have both incomes and voting, though in the case of groups it would be totals
or averages. The choice of which unit to use in testing a hypothesis
is extremely important. In the example just given, the relationship
between income and turnout may be very different, depending on
which unit of analysis is used.

One of the major pitfalls that can occur if the wrong choice of
unit of analysis is made is committing the *ecological fallacy: erroneously drawing conclusions about individuals from data on
groups*. This error is well illustrated in a paper submitted by a student in a political science class at Illinois State University. The student collected data on counties in the Southern states for a number
of variables and computed correlations for all the variables. One of
his findings was a strong positive relationship between the proportion of a county's population that was African American and

BOX 2.2 Examples of Hypotheses, Identifying Independent, Dependent, and Control Variables and the Unit of Analysis

1. Urban areas have lower crime rates than rural areas.
   Independent variable: Urbanization
   Dependent variable: Crime rates
   Unit of analysis: Geographic areas, such as states or counties

2. With age held constant, education and political participation are positively related.
   Independent variable: Education
   Dependent variable: Political participation
   Control variable: Age
   Unit of analysis: Individuals

3. The more negative the advertising in a U.S. senatorial campaign, the lower the voter turnout rate.
   Independent variable: Negativity of campaign advertising
   Dependent variable: Turnout rate
   Unit of analysis: U.S. states

4. With GNP held constant, communist nations spend more than capitalist nations for the military.
   Independent variable: Type of economic system
   Dependent variable: Military spending
   Control variable: GNP
   Unit of analysis: Nations

5. The better the state of the economy, the greater the proportion of votes received by the party of the president.
   Independent variable: State of the economy
   Dependent variable: Proportion of votes for incumbent party
   Unit of analysis: Elections

continues

---

continued

6. Controlling for political party, a legislator's votes
   on abortion are related to his or her religion and
   education.
   Independent variable: Religion, Education
   Dependent variable: Votes on abortion
   Control variable: Political Party
   Unit of analysis: Legislators

---

the proportion of the vote in the 1968 presidential election that
was received by George Wallace, the American Independent Party
candidate. The student concluded that it was African Americans
who voted for Wallace—an amazing finding since Wallace was a
well-known segregationist who opposed civil rights legislation.
This conclusion also contradicted the surveys of the time, in which
almost no minorities reported voting for Wallace.

This strange outcome was a result of the ecological fallacy.
The student's data and statistics were correct; indeed, others
have found that areas in the South with higher nonwhite populations voted more for Wallace. His error lay in drawing conclusions about which individuals cast which votes. It may be
that 30 percent of a county was African American and that 30
percent of the vote went to a particular candidate, but this tells
us nothing about how African Americans voted. This example
should serve to remind us of the importance of using the appropriate unit of analysis for testing hypotheses and drawing
conclusions. Committing the ecological fallacy may often be
tempting, because data on groups, such as populations of geographic areas, are much easier to obtain from published sources
than data on individuals, which usually must come from surveys. The best way to avoid the problem is to draw conclusions
only about the units of analysis for which the data were actually collected. If the data concern states, draw conclusions only
about states. The decision about the appropriate unit of analysis becomes crucial at the next step of the research process, in
which we construct operational definitions.

Operational Definitions

Testing hypotheses requires precise operational definitions specifying just how each variable will be measured. Operational definitions are a crucial part of the research process. If a variable cannot be operationally defined, it cannot be measured, the hypothesis cannot be tested, and the research question may have to be modified or even abandoned entirely. You will be better able to construct operational definitions after learning the material in later chapters, particularly Chapters 4 and 5, but the material here is critical to getting started.

Operational definitions have almost nothing in common with the definitions one finds in a dictionary. Whereas a dictionary might say that "race" refers to "any of the major biological divisions of mankind, distinguished by color of texture and hair, color of skin and eyes, etc.," an operational definition could be "ask survey respondents whether they consider themselves to be African American, White, Hispanic, Asian American, Native American, or other." Or, if the unit of analysis were a state, the operational definition might be "the percentage of the population that is nonwhite, according to the U.S. census of 1990."

As suggested in the previous section, the unit of analysis will often determine how a variable is operationalized, so it is necessary first to determine what the appropriate unit is for the hypothesis. Often the unit of analysis will be individuals, that is, people for whom data are available on each of our variables, so that we will eventually be able to compare the frequency with which individuals who have one characteristic also have another. Data on population groups, such as census figures and voting totals for cities and states, will not suffice. On the other hand, if our units are population groups, or *aggregates*, then those group data would be appropriate. A fundamental principle to be remembered is that *all variables in a hypothesis must be operationalized for the same unit of analysis.*

After the unit of analysis has been selected, constructing an operational definition has two requirements. It must specify precisely *what we want and where (or how) we will get it.* In the example of race for individuals used above, what we want is to know which ethnic group each person identifies with, and how we will get it is through a survey. If the same hypothesis concerned states, then what we would want for race would be the proportion of the population that is nonwhite, and where we would get it could be the U.S. Bureau of the Census.

As this example suggests, two units of analysis are very common in political science, and each has a typical type of data source. If the unit of analysis is the individual, meaning people in general, then the source usually must be a survey, for there are very few pieces of politically relevant information about ordinary people that can be obtained in other ways. The methodology of surveys will be presented in Chapter 5. However, if the "individual" is a special type of person, such as the holder of a government office, then many other variables are readily available. For example, for members of Congress, personal history data, campaign contributions and spending, and votes on legislative issues are a matter of public record. "Individuals" as a unit of analysis can also be institutions, such as interest groups, corporations, and political parties; often sources may be found of information already collected on them, though surveys of institutions may also be necessary.

Data sources for geographic population groups and governments at all levels are discussed in Chapter 4. An astonishing variety of information is collected by governments across the world as well as by other agencies. However, one principle to keep in mind when constructing operational definitions using data on groups is that the data usually must be *standardized*. This means that it should be measured in a way that makes comparison of different cases meaningful, usually by standardizing to the population. Unstandardized measures usually reflect the total size of the population group more than anything else. Thus if the variable is "how Democratic a state voted," the appropriate measure would be the percentage of the vote that was Democratic, not the total number of votes. If we are concerned with the wealth of nations, then per capita gross national product (GNP) would be a better measure than total GNP. (If we do not standardize these aggregate measures, then almost any variable will correlate with any other, simply because larger states or nations have more of almost everything than smaller ones.)

Box 2.3 presents examples of hypotheses and of how the variables might be operationalized. Exercise B at the end of the chapter presents other examples for self-testing.

**BOX 2.3   Examples of Hypotheses and
Operational Definitions**

1. The more a congressional candidate spends, the more
successful his or her campaign.

    Spending: The amount of campaign spending re-
    ported to the Federal Election Commission.

    Success: The percentage of the total votes received by
    the candidate according to *America Votes.*

2. The more economically developed a nation, the lower
the level of political instability.

    Economic development: Per capita GNP as reported
    by the *United Nations Yearbook.*

    Political instability: The average number of coups
    d'état, assassinations, and irregular executive
    transfers per year since 1970, according to the
    *World Handbook of Political and Social Indi-
    cators.*

3. The higher the level of a person's education, the more
likely he or she is to favor legal abortion.

    Education: Ask a survey respondent, "How far did
    you go in school?"

    Opinion on abortion: Ask the survey respondent,
    "Do you believe that abortion should be legal
    under any circumstances or not?"

continues

---

continued

   4. The more competitive political parties are in a state,
   the more the state spends on education.

   Party competition: The difference between the Republican and Democratic percentages of the vote
   for governor subtracted from 100, calculated from
   data in *America Votes*.

   Spending for education: Per pupil spending for public elementary and secondary education, according
   to the *U.S. Statistical Abstract*.

Exercises

Suggested answers for these exercises appear at the end of the
chapter. It is suggested that you attempt to complete the exercises
before looking at the answers.

Exercise A

For each of the following hypotheses, identify what appear to be
the independent, dependent, and (if any) control variables and the
unit of analysis.

   1. Media attention is necessary for a candidate to succeed in a
   primary election.
   2. With education, income, and region held constant, there is
   little difference in turnout between whites and African
   Americans.
   3. Southern states have less party competition than Northern
   states.
   4. When length of time since independence is held constant,
   democracies are more stable than dictatorships.
   5. The larger a city, the higher the crime rate tends to be.

Exercise B

For each of the following hypotheses, construct operational definitions for the variables.

1. Controlling for education, the more urban an area, the lower the voter turnout.
2. People who perceive that they are better off economically tend to vote for the incumbent candidate for president.
3. Nations that receive U.S. foreign aid are more likely to support the United States in foreign policy.
4. Winning candidates have more positive perceptions of voters than do losing candidates.
5. The better the state of the economy, the better the candidates of the incumbent president's party do in congressional elections.

Suggested Answers to Exercises

Exercise A

1. Independent variable: media attention; dependent variable: election success; unit of analysis: candidates
2. Independent variable: race; dependent variable: voter turnout; control variables: education, race, region; unit of analysis: individuals
3. Independent variable: region; dependent variable: party competition; unit of analysis: states
4. Independent variable: type of government; dependent variable: stability; control variable: time since independence; unit of analysis: nations
5. Independent variable: size; dependent variable: crime rate; unit of analysis: cities

Exercise B

1. Education: The median years of education of persons 25 years of age and over, according to the *U.S. Statistical Abstract*.

   Urbanization: The proportion of persons living in places with populations of 2,500 or more, according to the U.S. Bureau of the Census.

   Voter turnout: The proportion of persons of voting age casting ballots in the 1996 presidential election, according to the *U.S. Statistical Abstract*.

2. Economic perception: Ask survey respondent, "Do you think you and your family are better off economically, worse off, or about the same as you were four years ago?"
Presidential vote: Ask survey respondent, "Did you vote for Bill Clinton, Bob Dole, Ross Perot, or someone else in the election last November?"

3. Foreign aid: Did a nation receive any military or economic assistance from the United States in 1997, according the U.S. State Department?
Support in foreign policy: Percentage of time a nation voted with the United States in the United Nations General Assembly in 1997, calculated from data in the *United Nations Yearbook*.

4. Positive perceptions: Interview candidates for the state legislature and ask, "Do you think that voters in this district are highly informed, somewhat informed, or not very well informed about the issues?"
Winning/losing: Look at the report of the State Election Commission to see which of the candidates won the election and which lost.

5. State of the economy: The change in real per capita disposable personal income for the year of the election, according to the *Annual Report of the Council of Economic Advisers*.
Success of the incumbent president's party: Calculate what percentage of House seats were won by that party's candidates in each election from results in *Congressional Quarterly Weekly Report*.

3

Research Design

Once we have selected a research question and set forth one or more testable hypotheses, the next step is to formulate a research design. This step, along with the building blocks covered in the previous chapter, is critically important in the research process.

People use the term *research design* in two different ways. In this chapter, research design refers to the *logical method by which we propose to test a hypothesis*. But in a broader sense research design can refer to a whole proposal for a research project that would also include the review of the literature, details of how data will be collected, a discussion of the statistical tests that will be used once the data are collected, and possibly even a budget for the proposed expenditures. This broader sort of research design is what you would submit if you were asking for financial support for a project or approval for a graduate thesis proposal.

The Concept of Causality

The types of research designs presented in this chapter are all intended to test whether one variable *causes* another or *causes* the variation in another. As explained in the previous chapter, many hypotheses use the language of causation—for example, "influences," "leads to," or "is a result of." The previous chapter introduced the idea of an independent variable (the cause) and a dependent variable (the effect). Here we will see more completely what this idea of causality means and how it can be determined.

In order to draw the conclusion that one thing causes another, we must determine that three criteria have been met. The first is *co-*

variation, that is, evidence that two phenomena tend to occur at the same times or for the same cases. If we observe, for example, that every time there is a crisis in foreign policy, presidential popularity increases, or that people with high incomes are more likely than poor people to be Republicans, we are noting evidence of covariation. Covariation is also called *correlation*, and statistics that measure the strength of covariation are referred to as *correlation coefficients*—or simply *correlations*. All types of research designs intended to determine whether causation exists are set up to measure the extent of covariation.

People sometimes have stopped there and assumed that covariation alone is grounds for concluding that causation exists. This kind of reasoning can lead to the conclusion, for example, that storks are responsible for babies or that umbrellas cause rain. But, as is often repeated in methodology courses, correlation does not mean causality. Two other criteria must also be met. One is *time order*. We must have evidence that the presumed cause (the independent variable) happened before the presumed effect (the dependent variable). The third criterion is *nonspuriousness*. We must be sure that any covariation we observe between the independent and dependent variables is not caused by other factors. As we will see, each type of research design attempts to fulfill these criteria, with varying degrees of success.

Types of Research Design

The "True" Experimental Design

When many people think of "science," they think of experiments. It is true that the physical and biological sciences and some of the social sciences use experimentation frequently, though never exclusively. It is important to understand how an experiment is set up, not because experiments are terribly common in political science, but because the logic involved is relevant to all types of research design. We sometimes use the modifier "true" because the term *experiment* is sometimes used to describe all sorts of things that are not experiments at all.

Figure 3.1 presents an outline of what is required by the "classic" experiment—the simplest version of a true experiment. Experimentation has its own vocabulary, employing such terms

FIGURE 3.1   The classic experiment and an example

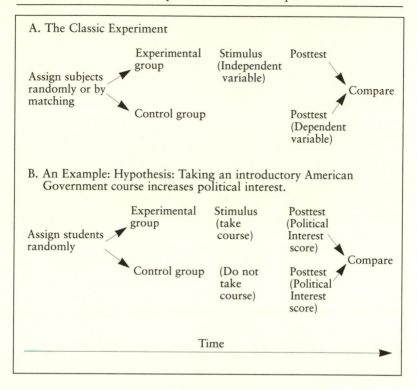

A. The Classic Experiment

Assign subjects
randomly or by
matching

Experimental
group

Stimulus
(Independent
variable)

Posttest

Control group

Posttest
(Dependent
variable)

Compare

B. An Example: Hypothesis: Taking an introductory American
Government course increases political interest.

Assign students
randomly

Experimental
group

Stimulus
(take
course)

Posttest
(Political
Interest
score)

Control group

(Do not
take
course)

Posttest
(Political
Interest
score)

Compare

Time

as *subjects* and *stimulus*; we will use them, but we will also see how they are translated into the terms we have used to describe hypotheses.

The classic experiment starts with a group of *subjects*, that is, the *units of analysis*, whether individual people, laboratory animals, or anything else. These subjects or units are then divided into two groups by some method that would assure that the two groups are as identical as possible on the dependent variable in the hypothesis. The best way to do this is to *randomly assign* the subjects to the two groups by some method such as flipping a coin. If this is done, then the two groups should, statistically, be identical in their distribution on not only the dependent variable but also on any other variables, whether or not those variables can be measured. Sometimes randomization is not used, mainly because the number of subjects in the experiment is too small. Under those circumstances it is necessary to use a *pretest* to measure the dependent variable. Then a procedure called "matching" is used to divide the subjects into two groups that have very similar distributions on the dependent variable.

The subjects in the first group, often called the *experimental* or *treatment group*, then receive a *stimulus*. The stimulus (or lack of it) is the independent variable in the hypothesis. The other group, called the *control group*, does not receive the stimulus. After the stimulus has had time to work its expected effects, all subjects in both groups are given a *posttest* that measures the dependent variable. Finally, the results of the two groups' posttests are compared. If they are significantly different in the way predicted by the hypothesis, then we can conclude that the hypothesis is confirmed. ("Significantly" is a statistical term that will be explained later in the book.)

To understand how the classic experiment can "prove" the hypothesis, it is useful to see how the three causality criteria are met. First, it is the *posttest comparison* that shows whether there is covariation. If, for example, the experimental group measures higher on the dependent variable in the posttest, then we see that the subjects who received the stimulus measure higher on the test than those who are not. Second, we must be certain that the results are nonspurious. This is assured by the fact that the experimental and treatment groups were exactly the same in all ways before the stimulus was applied. That is why it is so important that the subjects be assigned to groups by an appropriate method, such as randomization or matching. If they were assigned to groups in any other way, then we could not be sure that any difference between groups was caused by the stimulus. (It is also assumed that all subjects were treated in the same way in all other regards.) Finally, the criterion of time order is clearly satisfied by the fact that the stimulus (independent variable) is applied *before* the posttest measures the dependent variable. Thus, a properly conducted experiment can provide a convincing test of a hypothesis that one variable causes—or has a causal effect on—another.

Let us see how the classic experiment could be used to test the hypothesis that taking an introductory American Government course increases the degree of political interest among college students. (This example is also diagrammed in Figure 3.1.) First of all, we might take as our subjects all of the incoming freshmen at a college one year. Using the university's computer, we randomly separate them into two groups. We schedule one group (the experimental group) to take the course (let's call it PS 101), whereas those in the other group (the control group) are not allowed to take the course. At the end of the semester, we require every freshman to fill out a questionnaire that asks a list of questions about their interest in politics. The questionnaire, which is the posttest in this experiment, is structured such that the responses yield a score reflecting degree of political interest. If the experimental group—the group that took PS 101—has a higher average score than the control group, then we conclude that PS 101 caused greater interest, confirming our hypothesis.

It is important to emphasize that *manipulation of subjects* is a necessary part of any true experiment. In the PS 101 example, we had to tell students whether or not they would take the course, rather than allowing them to make that decision. Such manipulation is necessary because self-selection would probably yield two groups that would not be identical in their political interest initially. Indeed, students who have more interest in politics are more likely to choose to enroll in American Government, so the fact that they have more interest after taking the course than those who did not take the course would prove nothing in itself.

Although true experiments are generally considered to be the best test of hypotheses, they are also subject to a number of practical limitations. One of the biggest problems is that it is difficult or impossible to manipulate many independent variables. We cannot change a person's gender, race, age, or many other social characteristics or people's beliefs or attitudes. Nor can we manipulate larger social phenomena, such as wars, economic conditions, elections, or other events. In fact, the use of experimentation in political science has largely been limited to investigations of communications, for we can manipulate, at least temporarily, individuals' exposure to such stimuli as campaign speeches, advertising, news reports, and instructional events such as lectures.

Another problem with experimentation is a lack of representative samples. Whereas nonexperimental researchers usually make a careful effort to use random samples of the entire adult population for surveys, it is rarely possible to involve anything like a sample of the general public in an experiment. Typically researchers conducting an experiment advertise for people willing to spend a few hours of their time at a specified location participating in a study in exchange for a modest fee, but this inevitably will exclude large segments of the population. In the PS 101 example this was not a problem, since the relevant population consisted only of college students.

Another frequent problem is that experiments often are conducted in an artificial setting. Consider the typical situation in experiments on effects of the mass media: Most people do not usually watch television in a strange place, surrounded by strangers, knowing that they will have to fill out a questionnaire afterward. Indeed, the experiment may require watching material about politics by people who would never expose themselves to such stimuli on their own. Hence we can never be completely sure about whether the effects observed in the experimental situation would be the same in real life.

A related problem is that of outside influences. Most experiments in political science use human beings as subjects, and human beings cannot be as closely controlled as laboratory animals. Thus it is always possible that other stimuli, such as conversations, news events, and personal experiences, might affect some subjects. If the time between the stimulus and the posttest is minimal, as it might well be in a highly artificial setting, then this concern is minimized. But if the experiment runs for weeks or months, as in the PS 101 example, there are innumerable possibilities for other influences to exert an effect and contaminate the experiment. It is often a dilemma for the researcher as to whether to construct a limited, well-controlled experiment in a highly artificial setting or to use a real-world setting over a longer period and run the risk of having external influences affect the outcome.

Finally, ethical considerations are of particular concern in human experimentation. Unlike other research designs, in which subjects are only observed, presumably with minimal or no disturbance to them, experiments do something to subjects that they might not otherwise experience. This is obviously a serious consideration in biological, medical, and even some psychological research, where stimuli or other experimental conditions (such as the withholding of medical treatment) could be very harmful. It is seldom a serious problem in political science experiments, where stimuli usually are limited to communications, but possible dangers must always be considered. Indeed, federal law requires that research involving human subjects undertaken by any institution receiving federal funds (which includes almost all colleges and universities) be approved by a local panel. (The rule even extends to nonexperimental research involving any contact with individuals, including survey research.)

Despite all these potential problems, experimentation does have considerable merit as a technique for testing hypotheses. Indeed, every method has its limitations. The preceding discussion should serve to point out that although experiments are logically the best way to fulfill the causality criteria, in many situations they are not the best choice of research design.

A number of variations in experimental design expand on the simple classic model to circumvent some of the potential problems. One addresses the possibility that giving a pretest may have an effect on the subjects. If the subjects are initially given a questionnaire on some political topic, that alone may increase their interest or affect their opinions and thus potentially influence their responses on the posttest given an hour or two later. A solution to this problem is the *Solomon four-group design*, in which the experiment is done twice, once with pretests and once without. Posttest comparison can then determine the effect of the pretest as well as that of the stimulus. The Solomon four-group design is actually a version of the *factorial design*, which is used when there is more than one stimulus (and thus more than one independent variable) or differing levels of the same stimulus. The experiment is simply done two or more times with different subjects, so that each possible combination of stimuli can be applied. An example would be a study on the effect of precinct-level campaigning in which one group of subjects were exposed to political appeals only by Democrats, one only by Republicans, one by both parties, and a control group that received no appeals. Regardless of the number of groups and combination of stimuli, the logic of an experiment is the same.

The Quasi Experiment (Natural Experiment)

The second type of research design is commonly called the quasi experiment or natural experiment. This is an unfortunate label as it is not a true experiment. It can be presented in much the same terms as a true experiment, but it is often used without any such references. A better name might be the before-and-after design, for that is the essence: comparison of the dependent variable before and after the independent variable has been applied.

Figure 3.2 diagrams the quasi-experimental design. It does look similar to the classic experiment, but it differs in two vital ways. First, the subjects are not assigned to groups. Rather, we observe which subjects have something happen to them and then go back and sort them into the experimental and control groups. Thus the quasi experiment lacks manipulation of the independent variable, which is the essence of a true experiment. Second, the quasi experiment requires a pretest of the dependent variable, so that the amount of change can be measured for each group. It is a significant difference in change between groups that would lead to a conclusion that the independent variable influences the dependent variable. In this way, the criterion of *covariation* is met in this design. We can observe whether the stimulus (i.e., the independent variable) is associated with a different amount of change in the dependent variable.

But what about the other two criteria? The criterion of time order is met, as this before-and-after design always includes a measure of the dependent variable after the stimulus—and so we always know that the independent variable came before the dependent variable. But what about the criterion of nonspuriousness? A true experiment assures nonspurious results by starting out with identical experimental and control groups. But in the quasi-experimental design, the two groups may be (and usually are) quite different from one another in many respects. The quasi experiment relies on the assumption that all of the other possible factors, known and unknown, that might influence the dependent variable have had their effects on *all* subjects at the time of the pretest, and therefore any differences between the groups in the extent of change from pretest to posttest is presumed to result from the stimulus, that is, the independent variable. Admittedly, this assumption is something we can be less sure about than the principle that large, randomly assigned groups will be identical, as is the case in a true experiment. But it makes possible the testing of causal hypotheses in situations where a true experiment would be difficult or even impossible.

Figure 3.2 also outlines an example of a quasi experiment that is similar to the example of a classic experiment in Figure 3.1. The hypothesis to be tested is that watching a presidential debate increases intensity of support for candidates. The subjects are students enrolled in large sections of an introductory political science course. Before the debate, they are given a survey that measures

FIGURE 3.2   The quasi-experimental design and an example

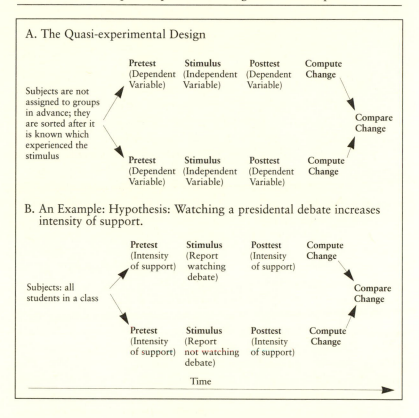

A. The Quasi-experimental Design

Subjects are not assigned to groups in advance; they are sorted after it is known which experienced the stimulus

| Pretest (Dependent Variable) | Stimulus (Independent Variable) | Posttest (Dependent Variable) | Compute Change |
| Pretest (Dependent Variable) | Stimulus (Independent Variable) | Posttest (Dependent Variable) | Compute Change |

Compare Change

B. An Example: Hypothesis: Watching a presidental debate increases intensity of support.

Subjects: all students in a class

| Pretest (Intensity of support) | Stimulus (Report watching debate) | Posttest (Intensity of support) | Compute Change |
| Pretest (Intensity of support) | Stimulus (Report not watching debate) | Posttest (Intensity of support) | Compute Change |

Compare Change

Time

their attitudes about the candidates, including which candidate they prefer and how strongly they hold that preference. After the debate, a second survey is administered, again asking for strength of preference and also asking whether or not the student watched the debate. The surveys include a coded means of identification so that the results of an individual's pretest can be compared with his or her posttest while guaranteeing confidentiality or anonymity. With matched pretests and posttests in hand, it is possible to calculate whether the intensity of candidate preferences increased more in those who saw the debate (the experimental group) than in those who missed the debate (the control group). Incidentally, a variety of studies over the years, including one by the author using this design, have generally confirmed this hypothesis. Presidential debates, it seems, do not generally make voters favor one candidate over the other; rather, they strengthen the preference for the choice the voter has already made.

The Correlational Design

The correlational design is very simple. At a bare minimum it requires only collecting data on an independent and a dependent variable and determining whether there is a pattern of relationship. However, it is usually advisable also to collect data on other potentially relevant variables and statistically control for them. Figure 3.3 presents an outline of this simple procedure. The correlational design differs from the quasi-experimental design in that it does not require any repeated measurements of a variable over time. (For that reason, it is also called a "cross-sectional" design.) It is by far the most common approach in political science research. To avoid confusion, it should be pointed out that "correlations," that is, statistical measurements of the strength of the relationship between variables, can be used not just in this type of design but also in quasi experiments and in true experiments.

How does this simple design fulfill the three criteria of causality? The extent of covariation is clearly determined by measuring the extent of correlation between the independent and dependent variables. The correlational design attempts to meet the criterion of nonspuriousness by analyzing the effects of control variables. This method is not as strong as that achieved by true experiments or even quasi experiments, because here we can control only for those variables of which we are aware and can measure. Although some correlational research may control for a considerable number of other factors, it is never possible to control for everything that might be relevant. However, it is often possible to ensure that some of the most prominent complicating factors are not creating a spurious relationship between the independent and dependent variables.

It is on the criterion of time order that the correlational design is weakest. Since no difference is required in the point in time when the independent and dependent variables are collected, we can never be sure that one must be the cause and the other the effect. However, as the discussion of independent and dependent variables in Chapter 2 pointed out, our knowledge of many subjects makes that determination fairly easy. We know that although a person's gender or race might affect his or her vote, it could not be the other way around. Hence, although the correlational design is fundamentally

FIGURE 3.3   The correlational design and examples

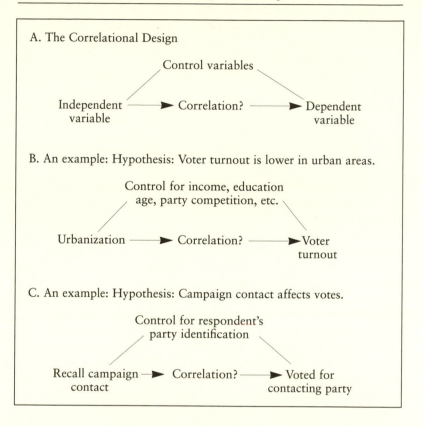

A. The Correlational Design

Control variables

Independent ———► Correlation? ———► Dependent
variable   variable

B. An example: Hypothesis: Voter turnout is lower in urban areas.

Control for income, education
age, party competition, etc.

Urbanization ———► Correlation? ———► Voter
turnout

C. An example: Hypothesis: Campaign contact affects votes.

Control for respondent's
party identification

Recall campaign ─► Correlation? ———► Voted for
contact   contacting party

weaker than the experimental and quasi-experimental designs, it
can provide considerable evidence of causality. And since it does not
require any manipulation or even continued measurements over
time, it can be applied in any situation where data can be collected
on two or more variables.

Here is an example of a correlational design (also diagrammed
in Figure 3.3). The author wished to test the hypothesis that voter
turnout is lower in urban areas. The units of analysis were counties within a state. The independent variable, urbanization, was
operationalized as the percentage of population living in "urban
places" according to U.S. census data. The dependent variable,
voter turnout, was simply the number of votes cast divided by the
voting-age population. When these two figures were analyzed, the

relationship was very apparent. The counties with no urban population had the highest turnout, and turnout declined as urbanization increased; the lowest turnout was in the metropolitan areas, which were almost entirely urban. But one might question whether it is really urbanization that affects turnout; after all, urban and rural areas differ on many other characteristics known to be related to turnout. Therefore, several other variables, all available from published sources, were used as control variables, including median income, median education, percentage employed in manufacturing, percentage in professional and managerial occupations, percentage nonwhite, median age, and a measure of party competition. When these other variable were controlled statistically (using multiple regression, a procedure that will be discussed in Chapter 10), the relationship between urbanization and turnout was only slightly diminished (Monroe 1977).

Correlational designs are frequently used in connection with data from surveys. Here is an example (also diagrammed in Figure 3.3) where a control variable proved to be important. The researcher (Kramer 1970) wished to test the hypothesis that contacting voters in a door-to-door campaign caused them to vote for the party that made the contact. The independent variable was measured by a survey question that asked whether the respondent remembered being contacted by any workers from either of the political parties before the election. The dependent variable was the respondent's reported vote. Analysis of these two variables revealed a definite pattern. Respondents who recalled having been contacted by Republican workers tended to vote Republican, and those who had heard from the Democrats usually voted for the Democratic candidate.

But did this mean that door-to-door contact really affected votes? When the respondents' party identification (i.e., whether respondents identified themselves as Republicans, Democrats, or independents) was used as a control variable, the relationship between contact and vote disappeared. What had happened was that party workers tended to contact voters who had supported their party in the past. Those people voted for the party of the contact, but they would have anyway. Like many other studies of campaigning, this example showed that such attempts to persuade voters rarely change their preferences.

The example also illustrates the importance of using control variables. Some correlational research reports can be found in which, for one reason or another, the analyst does not attempt to control for any variables. The results nevertheless have some value, because they tell us that two variables do occur together. However, our ability to draw any conclusions about causality between the variables is more limited. Methods of statistical controlling and their application to causal interpretation are presented in Chapter 10.

Designs That Lack Covariation

Although there are a great number of variations on these three basic types of design as well as ways of combining them, there is also a great deal of research in the literature of political and social science that does not meet the requirements of even a correlational design without control variables. Often this research does not involve quantitative data (though it could do so), but it may be quite empirical. Essentially, such work is descriptive and may serve to increase our knowledge, but it cannot "prove" anything in a scientific sense. An example of such descriptive work is the *case study*, in which the history of a particular event is recounted and analyzed, sometimes in great depth. There many examples of lengthy studies on how particular policy decisions were made. Their authors seek to shed some light on why those decisions were reached, but since only one case is studied, we have no way of knowing what the outcome would have been if conditions and actions had been different. The weakness of a case study is that it lacks the ability to measure covariation. Even if a case study could determine causality in some way, its conclusions would not be generalizations. However, case studies and other, similar types of research can be valuable because they may suggest research questions and hypotheses to which more rigorous designs involving larger numbers of cases can be applied.

Exercises

Suggested answers follow the exercise questions. It is suggested that you attempt to write these designs before you look at the answers.

Exercise A

Propose a hypothesis and a research design of the type specified.

1. Write an experimental design for the research question "Does negative political campaigning decrease voter turnout?"

2. Write a quasi-experimental design for the research question "Does increasing speed limits increase the number of traffic fatalities?"
3. Write a correlational design for the research question "Does election day registration lead to higher voter turnout?"

Exercise B

Propose hypotheses and write research designs of each type for the research question "Do the efforts of precinct workers contacting voters during a campaign gain votes for their party's candidates?"

1. Write an experimental design for this question.
2. Write a quasi-experimental design for this question.
3. Write a correlational design for this question.

Suggested Answers to Exercises

Exercise A

1. The hypothesis is that exposure to negative advertisements will decrease the intention to vote. Subjects are recruited by advertisements and offered $15 to participate in a study of local news. They are randomly assigned to the experimental and control groups. The experimental group is shown a videotape of a recent local newscast into which has been inserted an advertisement for a U.S. Senate candidate that is "negative" in nature, that is, it makes critical comments about the candidate's opponent. The control group watches a tape with the same content except that a nonpolitical product commercial has been inserted instead of the political ad. Afterward, the subjects are asked if they intend to vote in the Senate election or not. The percentages of each group intending to vote are then compared. This experimental design was used by Ansolabehere et al. (1994); the researchers also investigated the same research question with a quasi-experimental design using aggregate data.
2. The hypothesis is that increasing speed limits increases highway fatalities. When Congress allowed states to increase speed limits on interstate highways, some states did so and

others did not. This makes a quasi-experimental design possible. The pretest is the traffic fatality rate in each state during the last year that the speed limit was 55 miles per hour in all states. States are then divided into two groups: those that increased the speed limit during the next year and those that did not. The posttest is the traffic fatality rate in each state during the first year that some increased the limit. The changes in death rates from pretest to posttest for the two groups are then compared.

3. The hypothesis is that election day voter registration results in higher voter turnout. The units of analysis are states. The independent variable is whether or not a state had election day voter registration in 1996. The dependent variable is the percentage of voting-age population casting ballots in the 1996 presidential election. The relationship between these two variables is analyzed, controlling for other characteristics of each state's population, including median years of education, median family income, median age, degree of party competition, percentage living in urban areas, and whether it was a southern state or not.

Exercise B

1. The hypothesis is that people contacted by someone working for a candidate will be more likely to vote for the candidate. A random sample of registered voters is selected, and the sample is randomly divided into experimental and control groups. Workers go to the homes of voters in the experimental group and give a piece of Democratic party campaign literature to the selected voter and deliver a short speech asking for support for the candidate for Congress. Those in the control groups receive a nonpartisan brochure and message urging them to vote. Immediately after the election, the posttest is administered by using a telephone survey asking whether each person in the sample voted and, if so, for whom they voted. The percentages voting for the Democratic candidate supported by the campaign workers is then compared for the two groups.

2. The hypothesis is that voters who recall having been contacted by a campaign worker for a candidate will be more

likely to vote for that candidate. A random sample of registered voters is selected. A panel survey is conducted three months before a gubernatorial election, and all respondents are asked their voting intention in the coming election for governor. Immediately after the election, the same individuals are interviewed and asked for whom they voted. They are also asked if they recall having been personally contacted by workers for either candidate. The voting intention from the first survey for each individual is compared to his or her response from the postelection survey to see whether there was any change. The data are then analyzed to see whether there was greater change among those who were contacted by either party, contacted by both parties, or not contacted. Note that this is similar to the research by Kramer (1970) used as an example of a correlational design in Figure 3.3C. But the design proposed here is a quasi-experimental design because the dependent variable (voting intention) is measured both before and after the independent variable (possible contact by a party worker) is measured.

3. The hypothesis is that the more time put in by precinct workers for a party during an election campaign, the better that party will do in the election. The independent variable, worker time, is measured by surveying both the Republican and Democratic precinct committee members from a random sample of precincts in a state at the time of an election. They are asked how much time they put in during the campaign, and the net advantage in time to Republicans over the Democrats is computed for each precinct. The dependent variable is the Republican percentage of the vote for a minor office in each precinct. The relationship between these two variables is analyzed, controlling for other characteristics of the precinct available from census data, including median income, percentage in professional and managerial employment, percentage nonwhite, and median age. A number of studies have used this sort of design, including Katz and Eldersveld (1961) and Cutright (1963); most have found that precinct campaigning had only a small impact on the vote.

4

Published Data Sources

How do we get the data necessary to execute our research designs and test hypotheses? Often it is possible to use information others have collected and made available to the public. This is fortunate, because it is rare that even a very well funded project would allow the researcher to travel to many cities or states, let alone to all the nations of the world, to collect information first-hand. This chapter introduces some of the major published sources of data that political scientists use in their research and suggests some strategies for discovering other sources. The chapter concludes with a description of content analysis, a technique for turning verbal messages into quantitative data.

An explanation of the term *data* is needed here. Data might be defined as *empirical observations of one or more variables for a number of cases, collected according to the same operational definitions.* The examples of operational definitions presented in Chapter 2 included several that were based on published data from a reference source. When we have to rely on existing sources for our data, we must construct our operational definitions in terms of the data available. Having some familiarity with what kinds of data are available and where they might be found makes this task less difficult.

Although we usually think of data as numerical, this is not necessarily the case. Many variables are actually a record of which category a case falls into—for example, Republican, Northeastern, Catholic, high, medium, or low—but since the information found in published sources often concerns groups or *aggregates*, the data are in numerical terms, usually as totals or in some standardized form such as percentages or averages.

The Internet as Data Source

This chapter is mainly concerned with published data, which generally can be found in a library or, increasingly, on the Internet. In the sampling of data sources presented here, some Internet addresses are noted that can provide access to such sources. (The Internet addresses cited here were accurate at the time of this writing, but keep in mind that they may have changed.) Data obtained from the Internet should be used with caution, however, for several reasons. One is that since there is virtually no limitation, legal or practical, on what can be placed on the Internet, there are "data" to be found there that may be highly misleading, if not completely inaccurate. Probably the safest strategy would be to limit one's use of the Internet for research purposes to those sites that contain information such as government documents and standard reference books of the type one would find in the library.

Second, although searching for data over the Internet offers the advantage of not having to travel to a library, actually going to a research library (such as most college and university libraries), armed with the kind of background provided in this chapter, is likely to be much less time consuming than randomly searching Web sites. A major advantage of searching the Internet for data is the possibility of finding information that is more up-to-date than printed data.

The Importance of
Units of Analysis

As the discussion of hypotheses and variables in Chapter 2 should have made clear, the choice of unit of analysis is vitally important in planning a research project. This is especially true for research that relies on published data, as these data sources usually are organized by type of unit of analysis. Much of such data is reported by geographic or political units, such as nations, states, counties, municipalities, districts, census tracts, and precincts. In planning a research project that will use published data, it is necessary first to make sure that the information is reported for the particular unit of analysis needed. Often a given reference book includes data on many different kinds of variables (economic, political, social) but only for a single kind of unit, such as states or cities. Therefore, the presentation of major sources of data below is organized not only by the substantive type of data but also by the units for which the data are reported.

The sources suggested in this chapter are primarily of the type that would provide the information necessary for testing hypotheses. For example, if you wish to test a hypothesis about the relationship between the per capita income of nations and their level of voter turnout, you obviously need to find sources that report these data for a large number of nations, preferably almost all of them. If you had to rely on individual sources for each nation, your search would be much more time consuming, and you might well find that different sources use somewhat different definitions. Hence the sources suggested here report data for many cases, and often for all possible cases.

Most published data relevant to political research are aggregate data, that is, they report summary figures on the population of geographic or political units. Therefore, two reminders of points made in Chapter 2 might be useful here. First, one must be careful to avoid the ecological fallacy: Do not attempt to draw conclusions about individuals from aggregate data. Second, aggregate data usually are meaningful only if they are standardized in some way, such as in terms of percentages. Aggregate data often are already in an appropriate standardized form, but not always. Usually the researcher can convert the data into a useful form, such as by dividing a total by the population of the unit of analysis to produce the percentage or per capita figure.

Most published data are aggregate, but some are individual, mainly where the individuals are not ordinary people. For example, data on a number of personal characteristics of members of the U.S. Congress, including their individual votes on bills, is readily available. And "individuals" in the sense of unit of analysis can include government agencies, political parties, corporations, and unions, to name only a few institutions on which published data can be found. But in general, published sources provide little information of relevance to political research about ordinary people as individuals, though there is a great deal about groups of people. Therefore, it is sometimes necessary to collect such information not from a library but through an original survey, the methodology of which is presented in Chapter 5.

The following sections of the chapter, arranged by type of information and unit of analysis, are intended to introduce you to a few of the published data sources frequently used in political science research; it is just a sampling to get you started. Note also that the sources listed here are suggested only as places to find *data*. They would not be helpful in locating research findings or generally doing the background literature review necessary to formulate a research question.

Strategies for
Finding Data Sources

The resource to which many students turn first to find information in a library is the subject catalog. Although this is an appropriate resource for finding books that discuss research topics, it is not necessarily the most promising for locating data sources on those topics. Many of the most important collections of data, such as the *Statistical Abstract of the United States* (discussed below), include information on so many topics that not all would be included in the catalog. In addition, you will probably be interested only in a particular unit of analysis, such as states, so information on cities or nations would not be useful for you. Here are some tips that might lead you to what you need more quickly.

Gain Familiarity with Major Sources

The more familiarity you have with the important sources, whether you read them in the library or at an Internet site, the easier your search will be. This chapter is intended to provide the beginnings of that familiarity. Given the way libraries are organized, when you find one reference source, you may well find similar and possibly more useful sources nearby.

Look at Previous Research

As was emphasized in Chapter 1, it is important to review past research literature when formulating your research questions and hypotheses. The literature review is also useful for locating data, because you can see where others found their information. This tells you what was available and where it was found. However, to get this information, often you will need to go to the original report, typically a journal article, rather than relying on a summary, such as you might find in a textbook. Even when you have located a reference source, you may need to check the original source of its data for more detailed information, such as exactly how the variables were defined.

Consult Librarians or Other "Experts"

When at a loss for where to find information on a particular type of variable, consult the library staff. Most college and university libraries have personnel who specialize in different subject areas. Your questions are likely to be better received if you have thought out exactly what you need, including the unit of analysis. But be receptive for suggestions on alternative indicators for your variables. Consulting the library staff may be particularly important when using U.S. government documents, because libraries often catalog this material in different ways from other publications. Your library also may have databases on CD-ROMs, and some material may be available only on microfilm or microfiche, so advice from a staff member is particularly useful for the uninitiated.

Faculty members are another source of expertise. They have a great deal of experience with subjects in their disciplines and may be able to point you directly to the source you need. Much help is available if you ask for it.

Take Careful Note of the Sources You Find

Once you do find information that may fill your research needs, be sure to write down just where you found it, including all of the information about the publication. This is important for two reasons. First, you may need to consult that source again. Second, and more important, any research you present using those data will require a full citation of the source. Recording complete information is particularly important for Internet sites. Although bibliographic formats for citing electronic sources have not yet been standardized, it is certainly necessary to include the author (if available), the title, and the date as well as the exact site address and the date you accessed it (Scott and Garrison 1998, 123–124).

Some General Data Sources

A few sources encompass a number of categories of both types of data and units of analysis. *The Statistical Abstract of the United States,* published annually by the U.S. Department of Commerce, includes data on a wide variety of variables—political, demographic, economic, and social—for the United States as a whole and for the fifty states as well as a limited amount of information on U.S. metropolitan areas, major cities, and other nations. Although most of the information in the Statistical Abstract comes from the U.S. Bureau of the Census and other government agencies, it includes material from a wide variety of private sources as well.

Also worthy of mention is the *World Almanac,* which has been privately published every year for over a century. The *World Almanac* reports information on an enormous number of topics, and the latest edition will include some information more recent than other published books. It is also the most widely available reference book, and is reasonably priced and sold on newsstands.

The *American Statistics Index* is a comprehensive guide to data found in most U.S. government publications. It allows searches by subject matter as well as by geographic, economic, and demographic categories.

Internet site: Fedstats is an on-line source that provides access to statistical reports from many U.S. government agencies<http://www.fedstats.gov>.

Demographic Data

This section lists some sources of data on general population characteristics, including economic and social indicators—data such as income, employment, race, age, literacy rates, and government spending. The sources are presented in terms of units of analysis reported.

Nations

For the world as a whole and the nations as units, the primary sources are publications by the United Nations. The most general source is the United Nations Yearbook. More detailed information can be found in other UN volumes such as the *Demographic Yearbook, Statistical Yearbook,* and *UNESCO Statistical Yearbook.*

Note that the information on individual nations in these (and most other sources) is compiled from reports submitted by the governments of those nations. Therefore, it is always possible that there are considerable inaccuracies in some of the data, whether by design or by accident.

A number of other international agencies publish statistics on nations, particularly economic indicators. The International Monetary Fund (IMF) publishes the *International Financial Statistics Yearbook*. The World Bank publishes the *World Development Report* and *World Tables*. The Organization for Economic Cooperation and Development (OECD) publishes the annual *Economic Outlook*.

A number of private publications also report these kinds of data, usually drawing them from the more official sources, but often presenting them in a more convenient form. Examples include the annual *Statesman's Yearbook, Political Handbook of the World,* and *World Economic Data.*

U.S. States and Localities

The most convenient and comprehensive source for demographic, economic, and social data for states is the *Statistical Abstract of the United States,* described earlier. The basic source of almost all U.S. demographic information is the U.S. Bureau of the Census, which reports it in a number of publications. The census of the United States is conducted every ten years, and each census produces a set of volumes. Two overall volumes cover the nation as a whole and by state: *U.S. General Population Characteristics* and *U.S. Social and Economic Characteristics.* Separate volumes for each state provide more detailed breakdowns for units within the state, including counties and municipalities. Somewhat easier to use is the *County and City Data Book,* which includes a number of widely used variables for all counties and larger cities in every state, and the *State and Metropolitan Area Data Book,* which contains similar data for those units.

Internet site: The site for on-line census data is <http://www.cesus.gov>.

Privately published reference books for demographic data on states and units within them include the *Almanac of the Fifty States* and Kathleen O. Morgan's *State Rankings.*

A list of sources for other nations can be found in *The Statistical Abstract of the United States.*

Political and Governmental Data for Nations

This section lists a few sources of information about the governmental structure and politics for a large number of nations. This sort of data is generally not found in United Nations publications, which are, as noted earlier, based on information reported by the nations themselves. This is particularly true of indicators that might be used to measure variables such as political instability, democracy, and civil liberties.

Among the possible sources that report some of this political information are the *Political Handbook of the World, World Encyclopedia of Political Systems and Parties, the Statesman's Yearbook,* and the *International Yearbook and Statesman's Who's Who.* Particularly valuable for its data on variables such as assassinations, political rights, and irregular executive transfers is Charles L. Taylor and David A. Jodice, *World Handbook of Political and Social Indicators.* William D. Coplin and Michael K. O'Leary, *Political Risk Yearbook,* offers up-to-date assessments and predictions about likely political and economic conditions in all nations.

Of considerable interest to students of international politics are data on military and defense activities. Sources for this sort of data include Ruth Silvard, *World Military and Social Expenditures, World Military Expenditures and Arms Transfers, World Armaments and Disarmaments Yearbook,* and *Military Balance.*

The largest collection of international voting results data is Thomas T. Mackie and Richard Rose, *The International Almanac of Electoral History.* Kenneth Janda's *Political Parties* contains data evaluating parties and related topics for fifty-three nations.

Data on U.S. Government and Politics

This section lists a few of the most useful sources for finding information on the branches of the U.S. federal government as well as state and local units. One general, though hardly comprehensive, source is Harold W. Stanley and Richard G. Niemi, *Vital Statistics on American Politics,* which is designed for undergraduate students.

Congress and the Presidency

As American political scientists have probably devoted more time to studying the U.S. Congress than any other institution; a vast number of sources of data are available on the two houses, their members, and the districts they represent. The most basic source for Congress is the *Congressional Record*, published every day Congress is in session. The *Congressional Record* reports everything said on the floor (and text that is inserted "into the record" but was not said) as well as all of the votes cast by individual members. However, the *Congressional Record* is large and not particularly well organized, and a number of private publications are usually more useful for most research projects.

The most important references on Congress are the various publications of Congressional Quarterly, Inc. The basic source is the *CQ Weekly Report*, which includes news stories on what is happening in Congress and in government and politics generally as well as the votes of each member on bills and important procedural questions. If your research deals with past years, the annual *Congressional Quarterly Almanac* compiles much of the weekly information systematically. The biennial *Politics in America* provides profiles of members and their districts. *Congress and the Nation* is a set of books that compiles information over many years. Congressional Quarterly has long provided measures such as the presidential support score, a measure of how often Congress has agreed with the administration. A competing weekly publication is the *National Journal*, which is similar to *CQ Weeky Report* but concentrates somewhat more on the executive branch.

To track down the content and status of bills currently under consideration, the researcher may consult a Commerce Clearing House publication, the *Congressional Index*.

There are many other private publications on Congress. Particularly useful is the biennial *Almanac of American Politics*, which includes personal data on every member of Congress, their votes, their districts, their campaign finances, and ratings of their voting records by interest groups. John F. Bibby and Norman J. Ornstein's *Vital Statistics on Congress* assembles many useful sets of variables. More detailed data on campaign finance may be found in the *Almanac of Federal PACs* and Larry Makinson and Joshua Goldstein, *Open Secrets: The Dollar Power of PACs in Congress*.

The ultimate source for the data on congressional districts that appear in many of the aforementioned sources is a publication of the U.S. Bureau of the Census called *Population and Housing Characteristics for Congressional Districts*, which presents data in separate volumes for each state.

Many of the sources cited above for Congress, such as the *CQ Weekly Report* and the *Almanac* are also very useful for information on the president. Other sources include Congressional Quarterly's *Guide to the Presidency* and Lyn Ragsdale, *Vital Statistics on the Presidency*.

Internet sites: Information on the two houses of Congress, including documents and votes for recent years, may be found at <http://www.clerkweb.house.gov> and <http://www.senate.gov>.

State and Local Government

The most general source for data on state governments is the annual *Book of the States*, published by the Council of State Governments. Other sources include Kathleen O. Morgan, *State Rankings*, which deals mainly with spending; Kendra A. Hovey and Harold A. Hovey, *CQ's State Fact Finder: Rankings Across America*; and Alfred N. Garwood, *Almanac of the Fifty States*.

More detailed information may require reference to publications from individual states. The *Statistical Abstract* includes a list of major state sources, and M. Balachandran and S. Balachandran's *State and Local Statistics Sources* provides a detailed listing.

For local governments, the basic source is the *Municipal Yearbook*.

Election Returns

Results of federal elections—that is, for the presidency, the Senate, and the House—are relatively easy to find. Congressional Quarterly's *Guide to U.S. Elections* reports statewide and district figures for these offices since 1824. The *America Votes* series, published every two years since 1956, reports votes for federal offices and governor by county. *America at the Polls* does the same at the state level for the earlier years of the twentieth century. Walter Dean Burnham's *Presidential Ballots, 1836–1892* has presidential results by counties. The *World Almanac* provides county-by-county returns for recent presidential elections. Many of the general sources cited above, including the *Statistical Abstract*, also provide some state-level data.

Results for state and local elections are more problematic. Most state governments publish reports on each election for statewide and state legislative elections for the district and county level. For smaller units, such as wards and precincts, typically one must turn to local sources. Sometimes election results are published in local newspapers shortly after the election. But for precinct returns it may well be necessary to go to the city or county office responsible for administering elections to obtain such information. If you are contemplating a project that would require such localized election data, it is especially important to make sure that the data can be obtained before proceeding any further.

Survey Data

Although political science research frequently relies on survey data, most researchers are not in a position to conduct their own surveys on a large scale and must instead make use of the results of surveys conducted by others. The largest body of published survey results is found in the *American Public Opinion Index* and the accompanying *American Public Opinion Data*, which begin with 1981 data. The *Index* is just that, a topically arranged list of survey questions. To find out the answers to a question cited in the *Index*, one must then consult the *Data*, a microfiche collection of survey reports from a wide variety of sources.

A number of other sources are available. The Gallup Poll publishes *The Gallup Report* (monthly since 1965), which provides a breakdown of the responses to each question by a standard set of demographic variables. *The Gallup Poll* is a set of volumes going back to 1935 reporting all Gallup surveys in a more limited form. Elizabeth Hann Hastings and Phillip K. Hastings's *Index to International Public Opinion* (annual since 1978) reports surveys from the United States and many other nations. Floris W. Wood's *An American Profile* reports results from a number of questions repeated from 1972 to 1989 in surveys by the National Opinion Research Center.

Although published results of surveys from sources such as those cited above are necessarily aggregated, they can be used as sources of data for research designs that compare the results of different surveys. Examples of this type of research include the many analyses of how presidential popularity changes over time (e.g., Mueller 1973; Edwards 1983). There is also a body of research that uses results of surveys from many sources and combines this with data on government policy decisions to assess the relationship between public opinion and public policy (e.g., Page and Shapiro 1983; Monroe 1998).

Internet sites: Recent survey results from the Gallup Poll may be found at <http://www.gallup.com>. Other sites include the Princeton Survey Research Center <http://www.princeton.edu/~abelson/index>, The Odum Institute at the University of North Carolina <http://www.irss.unc.edu>, the Roper Center <http://www.ropercenter.uconn.edu/>, and the Social Science Data Archives-North America <http://www.nsd.uib.no/cessda/namer.html>. The National Election Studies, discussed below, may be consulted at <http://www.umich.edu/~nes>.

Political scientists also make considerable use of the individual responses to surveys conducted by others, thus allowing them to test hypotheses about individual behavior. Indeed, a large part of the research on voting behavior in the United States since 1948 is based on the National Election Studies (NES) conducted every two years by the Institute for Social Research at the University of Michigan. Data files containing the answers given by individual respondents to each of these extensive surveys are distributed through the Inter-University Consortium for Political and Social Research (ICPSR), an organization to which most universities and many colleges belong. The ICPSR also archives the results of hundreds of other surveys as well as other data sets, all available in computer-readable form. The ICPSR representative at a member institution should be contacted for further information. The complete set of NES survey data from 1948 to 1997 is available on CD-ROM.

Content Analysis

The sources cited in the previous sections provide information that is already in the form needed for data analysis or can be turned into a data set relatively easily. But often researchers in the social sciences wish to make use of information structured very differently, such as the text of speeches, news articles, or other documents. Is it possible to analyze such material in the same objective and systematic way as aggregate data, including the use of statistical analysis? In fact it is.

Textual data can be analyzed quantitatively through content analysis. This method has been defined as *"any technique for making inferences by objectively and systematically identifying specified characteristics of messages"* (Berelson 1971). Content analysis is most commonly associated with published verbal texts, but can also be used in conjunction with answers to open-ended questions on surveys.

Content analysis was developed in the early twentieth century and was first used for the analysis of newspapers. Later it was applied to propaganda, particularly during World War II. It has been used by researchers in many fields, including literature, linguistics, history, communications, and education as well as all of the social sciences. Examples from political science include the analysis of diplomatic messages (North et al. 1963), speeches by presidents, and political party platforms (Pomper 1980), and countless studies of news media content (e.g., Patterson 1980; Robinson and Sheehan 1983).

Content analysis is a valuable research tool that should not be overlooked in planning a research project. It is obviously appropriate and often essential if the research question deals with content itself, such as the question of whether news coverage of a political campaign is biased. But content analysis is also valuable as an indirect measure in situations where more direct observational methods cannot be used. For instance, we cannot interview the population from past generations, but we can systematically analyze what they wrote in speeches, letters, newspapers, and other documents.

Content analysis is a *data collection method*, not a type of research design. Indeed, content analysis can be used in conjunction with any of the research designs presented in Chapter 3. All of the usual stages in the research process apply when using content analysis, but some deserve particular emphasis. One is the importance of having a clear theoretical framework, research question, and hypotheses. These are highly advisable for any kind of research, but they are particularly important when planning content analysis, because failure to do so could mean that the whole process of analyzing a large amount of textual material is wasted effort. The steps that must be taken in a content analysis are the same as those in any other scientific investigation, but they have some slightly different twists.

Steps in Content Analysis

In the following explanation, content analysis will be illustrated with the example of a simple research question: Do newspapers give better coverage to incumbent candidates than to challengers? This question might produce two hypotheses. One is that newspapers tend to give more coverage to incumbent candidates for local office, and the other is that newspapers tend to give more favorable coverage to incumbents. These hypotheses could be tested with a correlational design. We would also need to control for other potentially relevant variables, such the party affiliation of each candidate for the offices we are studying.

Define the Population

We must first define the population, that is, *specify the body of content to which we wish to generalize.* In our example, we are obviously interested in newspaper stories about candidates, but in which newspapers—all newspapers, all daily papers, only papers with a circulation over a certain number, papers in a single state, or only one particular paper? Our decision would be based on the amount of time and effort we can devote to the content analysis as well as on how accessible the papers are to us. In this case we can, as discussed below, define a large population—say, all daily newspapers in the United States with a circulation of over 50,000—and then take a sample of that population—say, a random sample of twenty of those newspapers. Since we are not interested in everything printed in those papers, we must specify what kind of stories we will analyze. For our example, we might select all stories about candidates in any general elections for county offices. Finally, we must specify the time period to be covered. In this example, it might be from May to the November election in a particular year.

Select the Recording Unit

The recording unit is not necessarily the same as the unit of analysis that the hypothesis would seem to imply. Rather, it is *the segment of content for which data on the variables will be collected.* In this respect, content analysis is somewhat different from other data collection methods, because verbal texts can be divided several different ways.

The smallest recording unit in content analysis is the *word.* We can do frequency counts on the occurrence of individual words, such as how many times an individual's name is mentioned. However, the context in which a word is used is so important that longer units are frequently needed. Second, there is the *sentence* (or possibly the independent clause in a compound sentence). Each sentence could be classified on a number of variables. Pomper

(1980) used the sentence as a unit in his analysis of Republican and Democratic platforms from 1948 to 1976.

The most commonly used recording unit is the *item*, meaning a whole unit of communication. What constitutes an item can vary greatly depending on the type of communication being studied. With newspapers, the story is typically selected; in news broadcasts, it would also be the story or *segment*. An analysis of television entertainment programs, such as one investigating the amount of violence depicted, might well use the *program* as the recording unit. Although an item can be of any length, for most purposes very long items, such as whole books, are problematic because of the difficulty of classifying such large bodies of content.

Another possible unit is the *theme*. A theme is rather hard to define; it might be described as any occurrence of a particular idea that we are interested in. Themes might be used as recording units in analyzing, for example, a single book, but more typically we would record the occurrence and frequency of a particular theme within each recording unit.

These examples are just a sampling of the ways verbal content can be divided for the purposes of analysis. The choice of unit depends greatly on the type of content to be analyzed as well as on the research question to be investigated. In the example of newspaper coverage of local elections, we would select each *story* about candidates for county office as our recording unit.

Identify and Operationally Define the Variables

Next come the variables. In our two hypotheses, the independent variable is whether the candidate was an incumbent or a challenger. The dependent variables are the quantity of coverage and the quality of coverage. But there are several ways to operationalize each, and we might wish to use more than one.

The quantity of coverage is an example of a *structural* characteristic of a message, a relatively objective and unambiguous variable. We can measure the quantity of newspaper coverage in terms of the number of words or the length of the story in column inches. Broadcast news stories are usually measured in terms of time, that is, minutes and seconds. The length-of-story measure we select becomes our operational definition of quantity.

In our newspaper example, we might find it useful to measure other structural attributes as well, such as whether the story appeared on the front page or whether it was accompanied by a picture of the candidate. We would also need to record which candidate and office was the subject of the story, and it would be advisable to keep a record of which newspaper it appeared in, the date, and the page number, if only to make it possible to check for errors in data collection. We would have to know, preferably in advance, who all of the possible candidates were and which were incumbents.

The other dependent variable, quality of coverage, involves the *substantive* characteristics of a message. We might attempt simply to classify each campaign story as positive or negative toward the candidate, but this can be difficult to do. More useful would be first to specify the *categories* we will use to evaluate each story. After reading a good number of stories, we could identify the common categories of commentary about local candidates—experience, personal attributes, partisanship, and issues, plus the inevitable "other." Each of these categories would then be subdivided into comments that were positive, negative, and neutral toward the candidate in question. We should then attempt to specify the kind of words and phrases that would qualify for each subcategory. For example, "honesty" would be a positive personal reference.

Sample the Population

Whether or not we look at all of the content in the population we have defined is a question of how much time and other resources are available. In our example, we have already decided to look at a sample of twenty daily newspapers, but we might not have the resources to analyze all of the local campaign stories over a six-month period. Instead we can take a random sample of those stories. Random sampling is discussed in Chapter 5 in connection with survey research, but with content analysis it is usually a simple process, as we usually can identify all of the possible text material and specify where to find it. In the case of these newspapers, we know that they are published each day, so we could take a random sample of thirty days from each paper, either by using a random number table or simply by taking every sixth day. (It would not be advisable to take every seventh day, as that would give us the same day of the week every time.)

Collect the Data

We would then be ready to go through the selected issues of the newspapers. It would be advisable to prepare a form for the data collection, such as a sheet of paper that lists each variable, including all categories of the quality of the coverage. We would record that information for each story we found about a local campaign— this is referred to as *coding*. There are two ways to record the data on the various categories of positive and negative coverage. One is simply to record whether or not there were any references such as, for example, positive comments on experience. Slightly more time consuming, but more valuable, would be to record the number of references in each category. When we have finally gone through all of the selected newspapers and coded all of the relevant data, the information from our coding sheets can be entered into an appropriate computer program for analysis.

Analyze the Data

It is now possible to test our hypotheses. The methods of statistical analysis to be used will be described in later chapters, but we can preview some of it now. Data produced by content analysis, like any other data, can be evaluated in two general ways. First of all is *frequency analysis*, another name for univariate statistics (Chapter 6). Typically this entails simply tabulating how often different variables occur. In our example, frequency analysis would tell us such things as how much coverage the newspapers gave to the local campaigns and the extent to which it concentrated on the different categories of evaluation, such as issues and experience. But to test our hypotheses, we would have to perform *contingency analysis*, which is another name for multivariate statistics (Chapters 8 and 9). Contingency analysis would enable us to compare incumbent candidates and challengers on the quantity of coverage each received, as measured both in the number of stories and in their length in column inches, as well as the quality, as measured by the number of positive and negative comments each received. We could also control for the party of the candidate and the particular office being contested (Chapter 10). These analyses could be conducted for each newspaper as well as for the sample as a whole.

Issues in Content Analysis

An inherent problem in any content analysis, particularly that of the substantive variety, is *objectivity*. A decision as to whether or not a particular word or phrase falls into one of our categories is often somewhat subjective, that is, it may depend on the personal judgment of the person doing the coding at that moment. Although this problem cannot be avoided entirely, there are some steps that can be taken to minimize it. First of all, this is particularly a problem when several people are involved in the data collection. The solution is to have more than one person code the same subsample of text and then compare their results to see whether they coded the same material in the same way. The extent of the similarity of their decisions is called intercoder reliability and can be evaluated by several statistical measures. Even if one individual will be doing all of the data collection, the same approach could be used by having several other people code some of the same material to see if there are any subjectivity problems. It is also important to make as clear as possible what kinds of words and phrases should be included in each category. Finally, when the results of the content analysis are presented, it is important to include as many examples as possible of how actual statements were coded.

In using content analysis, as with many other methods of data collection, it is valuable to incorporate data from different sources. This is particularly important when a content analysis seeks to draw conclusions about the effects of communications. Thus researchers such as Patterson (1980) and Graber (1988) have combined surveys of individuals with content analysis of the news coverage to which their respondents were exposed. Pomper (1980) not only used the content analysis of party platforms to catalog the promises made by the parties but also used documentary sources to determine the extent to which those promises were fulfilled in later years.

Exercises

Answers to the exercises follow. It is suggested that you attempt to formulate solutions before looking at the answers.

Exercise A

Following are several variables that might appear in hypotheses. For each one, the unit of analysis is given. Your task is to devise an operational definition based on a published data source. This data source should be one that would provide the information for all or most of the possible cases. The exact data source should be cited with complete bibliographic information. In order to do this, it is necessary to actually look at that source to see exactly what information is available.

1. The level of mass political participation in U.S. states
2. Military spending of a nation
3. Liberalism of a U.S. representative's voting record
4. Economic development of a nation
5. Success of a U.S. president in dealing with Congress

Exercise B

Propose a research design using content analysis that could be used to investigate the research questions "To what extent have American party platforms increased their attention to the problem of crime over the years?" and "Have Republican platforms given more attention to crime than Democratic platforms have?"

Suggested Answers to Exercises

Exercise A

1. The percentage of the population eighteen years of age and older in each state casting votes for presidential electors in 1996. Source: U.S. Bureau of the Census, *Statistical Abstract of the United States, 1998* (Washington, DC: U.S. Government Printing Office, 1998), 298.
2. Military expenditures as a percentage of each nation's gross national product in 1996 (or latest year available). Source: Ruth Leger Sivard, *World Military and Social Expenditures, 1996* (Washington, DC: World Priorities, 1996), 45–47.
3. The rating given to each representative's voting record by the interest group Americans for Democratic Action in 1994. Source: Michael Barone and Grant Ujifusa, *The Almanac of American Politics 2000* (Washington, DC: National Journal, 1999). (Data on individual representatives are found throughout the book.)

4. The per capita gross domestic product (GDP) of each nation. Source: *The World Almanac and Book of Facts, 1999* (Mahwah, NJ: World Almanac Books), 760–861.
5. Average percentage total House and Senate concurrence. Source: Lyn Ragsdale, *Vital Statistics on the Presidency*, revised edition (Washington, DC: Congressional Quarterly, 1998), 390–391. (These data are available only from 1953 on.)

Exercise B

The hypotheses to be tested could be that parties have given more attention to crime since 1980 than they did in the 1960s and 1970s and that Republican platforms tend to give more attention to crime than Democratic platforms. The unit of analysis would be the Republican and Democratic platforms since 1960, the texts of which can be found in the annual *Congressional Quarterly Almanac* for each presidential election year and also in the *CQ Weekly Report* after each national party convention.

The content analysis could be conducted in several ways. The recording unit could be the sentence, in which case one would count the number of sentences in which some reference to crime appears. Alternatively, one could count the number of times the word "crime" (or a synonym) appears or measure the length of the sections dealing with crime (in words, lines, or inches). Whatever method is used, the measurement should be *standardized*, that is, computed in comparison to the total number of sentences, words, lines, or inches. This is important because party platforms vary in length, generally increasing over the years.

If these data were collected, it would then be possible to calculate whether relatively more attention was given to crime in later platforms than earlier and whether there was a difference between the political parties.

5

Survey Research

Survey research, also called "polling," means *taking a sample of a larger population, asking questions, and recording the answers.* Survey research is a such a common method of data collection—it is used not only in social science research but also in political campaigns and market research—that understanding how it is conducted is valuable for everyone. Survey interviews are used for large samples of the general population as well as for specialized groups such as holders of government positions. The logic of sampling is the same whether one is selecting citizens for a survey, laboratory animals for experimental and control groups, or anything else.

Sampling

Since researchers are usually interested in drawing conclusions about populations that are so large that it would be impossible to interview all of the individual members, they use samples. People sometimes express doubt that estimates based on only a tiny fraction, perhaps 2,000 out of a population of 200 million, can be accurate, but they usually are. Although this is demonstrated by long experience with surveys, such as election predictions, the rationale for sampling is mathematical, based on probability theory.

Suppose you were faced with the task of determining the relative number of red and black marbles in a very large basket. If you looked at only a single marble, that would tell you very little. If you started to draw more marbles out of the basket, a pattern would tend to emerge. By the time you had drawn 100 marbles, the percentages of red and black would resemble those of the whole basket. As the sample grew, the proportions would remain fairly constant but would come closer and closer to the proportions of the total. For accuracy, however, this process must be free of bias. The researcher cannot select more marbles of one color on purpose, and the basket should be well mixed beforehand. Such considerations are necessary to assure a "random sample." Note that the results are a matter of chance. Even if the basket is evenly divided in color, it is possible to draw a sample of ten red marbles or even a hundred, and no black marbles, though that is extremely unlikely.

The point of this example is that if sufficiently large random samples are taken from a population, they will tend to approximate the characteristics of that population. Furthermore, the distribution of these samples takes the form of a *normal distribution*—a bell-shaped curve—which allows us to estimate the accuracy of a given sample.

The larger the sample size, the more accurate the measurement is likely to be. Table 5.1 illustrates this principle. The column headed "95% Confidence Interval" shows the maximum amount of error a sample would make 95 percent of the time. In other words, for a sample of 1,000, we could be 95 percent sure that a sample would be off by no more than 3.1 percentage points in either direction. If we were taking a survey of how people had voted in an election in which the total vote was 55 percent Republican, then a sample of 1,000 should almost always come out between about 52 and 58 percent Republican. (On average—50 percent of the time—we would expect to not be off more than about one percentage point.) Note that the figures in Table 5.1 are based on several assumptions, the most important of which is that a simple random sample is used.

A frequently asked question is "How large should a sample be?" As noted above, the answer is "the larger the better," but this requires some qualification. As Figure 5.1 shows, the relationship between sample size and accuracy is not a straight line. Increasing the size of small samples considerably increases accuracy, but the relative gains diminish with larger samples. (This relationship occurs because the amount of sampling error is proportional to the square root of sample size.) However, the considerable costs of survey research are directly proportional to the number of interviews conducted. Hence even well-financed commercial surveys rarely exceed 2,000 cases unless there is some special need, such as a desire to obtain accurate measurements for subsamples of the population.

TABLE 5.1   Sample Size and Accuracy

Sample size	95% Confidence Interval (±%)
10	31.0
25	19.6
50	13.8
100	9.8
250	6.2
500	4.4
1,000	3.1
5,000	1.4
10,000	1.0

NOTE: These figures assume simple random sampling from an infinitely large population of a characteristic held by one-half the population.

Keep in mind also that the ranges shown in Table 5.1 are what could be considered the "maximum error," that is, nineteen times out of twenty (another way of expressing 95 percent), the survey will be more accurate than the interval shown. Samples of a few hundred or even fewer can be quite useful for many research purposes. One factor that makes little difference is the size of the population from which the sample is drawn. It is true that a sample of any given size taken from a single city will be more accurate than one drawn from the whole world, but unless the sample size is one half or more of the population size, the gain in accuracy is very small.

Sampling can be done in several different ways. A simple or pure *random sample* is a sample taken by a method ensuring that *each member of a population has an equal chance of being selected*. If we have a list of all of the members of a population, then there are many ways of selecting such a sample. If our population is the students enrolled at a particular university, then we could number them and use a random number table to select the needed sample; a computer could readily perform the same function. The name of each student could be placed on a slip of paper and the sample drawn from the figurative hat. A variation that produces essentially the same result is the *systematic sample*, in which a random start-

FIGURE 5.1   Sample size and accuracy

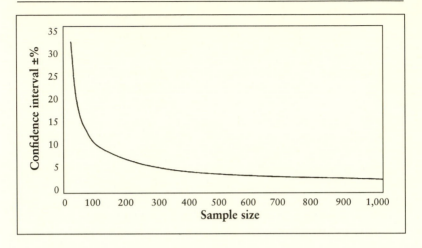

ing point is used and then every tenth name (or every hundredth, or whatever increment is needed) is chosen. In short, if a list of the members of a population is available, it is easy to select a random sample.

However, if the sample is to be drawn from the general popula-tion of the nation, or even from a particular city, such lists are not available. Because of that and other practical considerations, mul-tistage *cluster sampling* was developed for large surveys using per-sonal interviews. Cluster sampling involves sampling of geographic areas down to the city block, resulting in the selection of a number of "clusters" around the country where interviewing is done. For technical reasons, cluster sampling is somewhat less efficient than pure random sampling, so a survey that employs it, such as the Gallup poll, needs a sample of as many as 1,500 respondents to achieve the accuracy level of a pure random sample of 1,000. Large-scale telephone surveys that use *random digit dialing*, whereby telephone numbers are randomly constructed from the range of possible numbers, actually use a form of cluster sampling of area codes and exchanges.

Random and cluster samples are both *probability samples*, that is, *every case in the population has a known chance of selection*. A number of other methods are used that do not meet this test. In the "street corner sample" the interviewer stands in a public place and questions whoever will stop. In the "straw poll," individuals select themselves to be respondents. One version of the latter is the practice of encouraging people to phone in to express their opinions. Neither of these has any guarantee of relative accuracy, and they are not used for serious research, academic or otherwise.

The "exit polls" conducted by journalists on election day, in which interviewers approach people leaving the polling place, may appear to be a variation of "street corner sampling," but they avoid the usual bias of that approach in that everyone who is voting that day (aside from those casting absentee ballots) must leave a polling place. By sampling precincts and using a predetermined formula for what proportion of voters should be approached, it is possible to select a reasonably representative sample. The exit polls conducted by the television networks since 1980 appear to be highly accurate, at least in their estimates of election outcomes.

Interviewing

There are two ways that people can be asked questions, and each is commonly done by two different methods. In interviewer-administered surveys, the interviewer reads the question and records the response. This can be done in a personal (or face-to-face) interview, usually in the respondent's home, or over the telephone.

Personal interviews are generally considered to result in a higher quality of measurement than telephone interviews. Respondents in personal interviews have been found to be somewhat more at ease, to understand questions better, and to be more likely to express preferences. Personal interviews can be longer than telephone interviews, and visual displays can be shown to the respondent. However, personal interviews conducted by going door-to-door are extremely expensive, and so most surveys in recent decades have been done by telephone. Some degree of bias is built into this method, since some people do not have telephones, but today this is a relatively small problem. Telephone surveys also offer the advantages being conducted more quickly, presenting fewer problems of access (such as respondents unwilling to open their doors to strangers), and allowing more callbacks to households where no one was home, in comparison with personal interviews.

An alternative means of conducting a survey is the *self-administered survey*, in which the respondent reads the questions and records his or her own answers. One problem with this method is that a significant proportion of the adult population of the United States (as high as 30 percent by some estimates) has a low reading level. This means that some potential respondents will not be able to respond at all to a self-administered questionnaire, and many others will be reluctant to do so or not understand the questions.

One method of conducting self-administered surveys is to mail the questionnaires out and hope that the respondents return them. The great disadvantage of this approach is that response rates are typically very low. The lower the response rate, the greater the probable bias in sample selection. Those who do choose to participate may well be different from those who do not; for example, they may be those with more intense feelings about the survey's general topic. Response rates can be increased by including a cash payment or calling respondents to encourage their participation, but such steps erode the cost advantages of self-administered surveys.

The self-administered survey also has a potential sampling problem. In a well-done mail survey, questionnaires are sent by first class mail addressed to a specific respondent. However, since complete lists of the general population are not available, the mail survey is not a good approach for this population. Mail surveys can be more useful in researching specialized populations, such as members of an organized group or occupation. In these circumstances a list of the population is available and those sampled likely have greater interest and possibly above-average reading levels, leading to higher response rates. Even then, a well-done mail survey requires sending one or more additional waves of surveys and follow-up reminders to those who have not responded, and the project will necessarily take several weeks or months.

Another common method of conducting a self-administered survey is to use a *captive population*, that is, a group that is assembled for some other purpose and over whom the researcher has some minimal control. The most common example would be a classroom of students. People attending a meeting and employees on the job are other possibilities. The advantage of using a captive population is that it is inexpensive. The great disadvantage is that this method can never result in a random sample or even a representative sample of the whole population. However, it can be quite useful if the research question deals with a specific group whose members are available and willing to fill out a survey questionnaire.

Writing Survey Items

The most critical step in survey research is writing the questions, or *items*, to be presented to respondents. There are two basic types of questions: *closed-ended*, in which respondents are given all of the possible answers, and *open-ended*, in which respondents are given a more general question and asked to articulate their own answers. Most surveys consist of closed-ended items. This is not because closed-ended questions are better measurements, but because they are easier and less costly to administer, process, and analyze.

The case can be made that open-ended questions are often better for measuring the opinions, attitudes, and concerns of respondents. Most people will make choices on long lists of typical yes-or-no questions even if they have no preferences on those topics. But if they are given open-ended items, their real feelings can be expressed. The problem with open-ended items is that it is more difficult for the interviewer to record the responses and for the analyst to classify the responses into categories for tabulation. The latter process is actually a form of content analysis, discussed in Chapter 4.

Closed-ended items can take a variety of forms, with the yes-or-no, agree-or-disagree, or other dichotomies being the simplest. In an effort to measure more precise degrees of intensity, more complex sets of choices can be used, for example, "Do you strongly agree, agree, disagree, or strongly disagree?" When it is possible to show visual aids to respondents, various kinds of visual scales can be employed, in which respondents indicate where along the scale their opinions fall. Whatever the format, the answers to a closed-ended question should meet two criteria: They must be *mutually exclusive* and *collectively exhaustive*. In other words, the answers should not overlap, and the categories must cover all possibilities, so that anyone's opinion would fall into one of them.

There are a number of common problems in the construction of survey items. These are summarized in Box 5.1 along with examples and how the problems might be corrected. (Additional examples can be found in the exercise at the end of this chapter.) One of the most important considerations is that *respondents must be competent to answer a question*. This means that there is a reasonable expectation that most of the population to be sampled has some knowledge of the subject matter and terminology to be used. Asking members of the general public whether they favor passage of House Resolution 1314 is silly, even if the resolution refers to a prominent issue. However, it is permissible and often advisable to present a summary of a proposal before asking about preferences. In this way, all respondents are being asked about the same subject. Another technique is to use a *filter question*, whereby respondents are first asked whether they are familiar with a topic. The problem of competency arises not only with technical knowledge, but even with personal knowledge, as we cannot assume that most people know such things as the amount of income tax their family paid last year or the population of their own community.

An obvious requisite is to *avoid using any biased or emotional language* in survey questions. The choice of wording should be as neutral as possible so that the phrasing of the question does not sway the respondent to one side. Asking whether the death penalty should be used for "bloodthirsty killers who torture their innocent victims" is inappropriate and unnecessary. Although such extreme emotionalism is not likely to be used, the problem of bias can be more subtle when any controversial individual or group is unnecessarily introduced into a question, such as associating a political figure with a substantive policy proposal.

A common pitfall in writing survey items is failure to *avoid leading questions*—items that fail to present all of the possible alternatives. If we ask respondents only, "Do you agree with this proposal?" we are "leading" them into a positive response. Hence it is necessary to include phrases such as "do you agree or disagree," "do you favor or oppose," "would you say we should or should not." Because some respondents are eager to agree with an interviewer, it is especially important to make clear that negative responses are acceptable. Most surveys do not customarily present "no opinion" to the respondent as a possible choice, but interviewers should always be ready to accept it as a response and not attempt to force a choice.

In survey questions, *short and simple items are best*. If a question is long and complicated, it is harder for the respondent to understand what is being asked. Admittedly, some topics are more complicated and require more explanation, but the solution in such cases is to set forth the details, in several sentences if necessary, and then ask a simple question.

Another rule is to *never state questions in the negative*. For example, asking "Do you agree or disagree that the United States should not reduce its contributions to the United Nations?" is likely to be confusing to the respondent.

BOX 5.1   Rules for Writing Survey Items, with Examples

1. Respondent must be competent to answer.
   Wrong: "Do you think Section 14-B of the 1947 Taft-Hartley Act should be repealed or not?"
   Better: "At the present time, states can prohibit contracts that require workers to join a union. Would you favor or oppose taking away a state's power to prohibit such contracts?"

2. Avoid biased or emotional language.
   Wrong: "Do you favor or oppose the United States continuing to waste your hard-earned tax dollars on foreign aid?"
   Better: "Do you think that the amount of money the United States spends on foreign aid should be increased, decreased, or remain the same?"

3. Avoid leading questions.
   Wrong: "Do you agree that there should be term limits for all elective offices?"
   Better: "Do you agree or disagree with the idea that there should be term limits for all elective offices?"

4. Short and simple questions are best.
   Wrong: "Would you favor or oppose the idea that all employers be required to provide health insurance for all their employees meeting certain minimum standards, with the government providing health insurance for people who are unemployed?"
   Better: "It has been proposed that all employers be required to provide health insurance for all their employees meeting certain minimum standards. The government would provide health insurance for people who are unemployed. Would you favor or oppose this idea?

5. Do not state questions in the negative.
   Wrong: "Do you think the United States should not decrease its involvement in Bosnia or not?"

continues

76

continued

Better: "Do you think the United States should decrease its involvement in Bosnia or keep it at the current level?"

6. Avoid unfamiliar language.
   Wrong: "Is ideological proximity more important in your electoral decisionmaking than fiscal considerations?"
   Better: "Which is more important to you in deciding how to vote—how liberal or conservative a candidate is, or how the candidate stands on taxes and spending?"

7. Avoid ambiguous questions.
   Wrong: "Do you favor or oppose the proposal to improve education?"
   Better: "It has been proposed that all public schools test children in the third and sixth grades and the senior year in high school to make sure they have learned what they should. Would you favor or oppose this idea?"

8. Minimize threats.
   Wrong: "Do you want to keep black people out of your neighborhood?"
   Better: "Suppose a family who had about the same income and education as you were going to move into your neighborhood, but they were of a different race. Would this bother you or not?"

9. Avoid double-barreled questions.
   Wrong: "Should Central High School and North High School be merged and the new school be named Central or not?
   Better: "Do you agree or disagree with the proposal to merge Central High School and North High School? If the two schools were merged, should the new school be named Central or North or something else?"

An obvious consideration is vocabulary used: *Never use "big" words that would be unfamiliar to the average person*. Terms such as "ideological," "recidivism," and "philanthropic" might be appropriate in a college classroom, but certainly not in a survey. In almost all cases, language familiar to almost everyone can be substituted. If a technical term cannot be avoided, then it must be explained.

Ambiguous questions must be avoided. An ambiguous question is one that could have more than one meaning. This is a matter not only of the wording but also of the substance of the question. For instance, asking someone a question using the aphorism that "politics makes strange bedfellows" might cause some respondents to come up with some very interesting interpretations today. Even a reference to such familiar phrases as "Right to Life" and "Freedom of Choice" might be misinterpreted if it was unclear whether the question concerned abortion. A common reason for ambiguity is vagueness. It must be clear to the respondent just what the question is about.

Some survey questions may be threatening to respondents; *threats should be avoided, or at least minimized*. When asking about whether the respondent engages in socially unacceptable behavior, such as use of dangerous or illegal substances or exhibiting racial prejudice, there is a risk that the respondent will refuse to answer or, more likely, be less than honest. This problem can occur with less controversial topics as well. For example, asking whether a person watched the presidential candidate debates may seem to imply that they were not good citizens if they did not. The threat in this case could be reduced by asking, "Were you able to watch the debates or not?" This offers an implied excuse for those who did not watch, and it extracts the same information.

A final rule is *avoid double-barreled questions*. These are items that attempt to get one answer to two different questions, for example, "Do you think that the United States should reduce foreign aid and spend the money on welfare here at home?" These subjects can and should be covered in two separate questions.

Writing good survey items is a combination of good communication skills and experience. One way to help ensure that questions are clearly worded and unlikely to be confusing to respondents is to try the questions a number of times before administering the final version. Indeed, in well-done surveys researchers often select a sample of actual respondents for a pretest and conduct a small-scale survey in the same way they proposed for the actual project. As for experience, even novices can draw on the experience of others by looking at questions that have been used in other surveys. (Many of the sources of survey data presented in Chapter 4 include the wording of questions.) If your survey uses the same wording as another survey has used, you may gain the added advantage of comparing your results with those from a different sample. Even if the precise topic is not covered in another survey, similar wording can often be adopted. This is not to say that all published surveys, commercial and academic, are well written, but they offer a good starting point for the researcher in training.

Exercises

Exercise A

Following are some survey questions, each of which contains one or more of the common problems discussed in this chapter. Identify the problems in each and then write an improved version of the question that would avoid the problems.

1. Aren't you concerned about the state of the economy and in favor of the balanced budget amendment?
2. Do you think we should do more to reduce crime?
3. Do you think that people should be allowed to do things that are not good for them or not?
4. Do you agree or disagree that we should not get involved in the situation in Kosovo?
5. Do you think that those money-hungry tobacco companies should be severely punished for killing all those innocent people?
6. Which candidates for county office did you vote for in the election?
7. Should the United States use retaliatory tariff barriers to reduce our balance of payments deficit, or should we rely on bilateral negotiations?
8. Do you agree that the death penalty should not be used as a punishment for murder?

Exercise B

Suppose that you wished to test the hypothesis that the more education people have, the more liberal they tend to be on social issues. Propose a research design using survey research to test this hypothesis. You should specify the type of design you would use, details of the survey (population, sampling method, sample size, and interviewing method), and operational definitions of all variables (these will be the survey questions you would ask).

Suggested Answers to Exercises

Exercise A

1. This is a leading question and it is double-barreled. Improved: "How concerned are you about the state of the economy today—would you say that you are very concerned, somewhat concerned, or not very concerned at all?" "Do you favor or oppose the idea of an amendment to the U.S. Constitution that would require a balanced budget every year?"
2. This is an ambiguous question, as there are many proposals on this topic. Improved: "Do you favor or oppose longer prison sentences as a means to reduce crime?"
3. This is an ambiguous question, as the respondent would not know what kinds of "things" are being considered. Improved: "Would it be a good idea or a bad idea if smoking cigarettes were made illegal?"
4. This question is stated in the negative and also may raise questions of competency to answer, as respondents may not be familiar with this situation in the former Yugoslavia. Improved: "As you may have heard, there is a section of the former Yugoslavia called Kosovo, where most of the people are of Albanian ancestry and where the Serbian government has been accused of killing civilians. Do you think that the United States should send troops to try to keep the peace in the area or not?"
5. The question includes emotional language and it is leading. Improved: "Would you favor or oppose imposing heavy fines on tobacco companies to cover the costs of health care for people who smoked cigarettes?"

6. Respondents would not be competent to answer this question, because they would probably not remember their votes. Improved: "Did you happen to vote in the election last November for Sheriff?" "Did you vote for John Smith, the Republican, or Bill Jones, the Democrat?"
7. This question uses unfamiliar language. Improved: What should the United States do about the trade imbalance that comes of our buying more from other countries than we sell to them—should we raise our taxes on goods we import or should we try to work it out with those countries?
8. This is a leading question and is stated in the negative. Improved: "Do you agree or disagree that the death penalty should be used as a punishment for murder?"

Exercise B

The most appropriate design here would be a correlational design in which the independent variable is an individual's education, the dependent variable is the individual's degree of social liberalism, and control variables are the individual's age, social status, race, and religion.

The population to be surveyed would be the adult population of the United States. The data could be obtained by means of telephone survey using random digit dialing with a sample size of 1,500.

The respondent's education would be determined by asking, How far did you go in school—did you attend high school, graduate from high school, attend college, or graduate from college? Social liberalism could be determined by asking the following questions:

1. Would you favor or oppose adoption of a constitutional amendment that would make abortion illegal under any circumstances?
2. Would you favor or oppose making it illegal to discriminate against hiring someone because he or she was a homosexual?
3. Would you favor or oppose a constitutional amendment that would allow prayer in the public schools?
4. It has been proposed that the U.S. government make a payment to all African Americans to make up for what they suffered as a result of slavery in the United States. Would you favor or oppose this?

5. Would you favor or oppose stronger laws that would restrict the sale of pornography?

The answers to these questions would then be coded as to which was liberal (1, oppose; 2, favor; 3, oppose; 4, favor; 5, oppose), and each respondent then would be given a score equal to the number of liberal responses.

The control variables would be measured by answers to the following questions:

Age: How old are you?

Social status: Would you describe yourself and your family as generally being in the upper class, middle class, working class, or lower class?

Race: Would you describe your racial or ethnic status as white, black or African American, Hispanic or Latino, Asian American, or Native American?

Religion: Is your religion Protestant, Catholic, Jewish, or something else?

6

Statistics:
An Introduction

Once the observations of the variables in a hypothesis have been made and assembled into a data set, the next step in the research process is to analyze those data in order to draw conclusions about the hypothesis. However, the bits of data are often numerous indeed. This is particularly true in the social sciences, where we may have survey results on dozens of questions from hundreds or even thousands of respondents. To look over such a vast array of data to "see" what is there would be a very difficult task. In order to evaluate our data and determine what patterns are present, we need statistics.

There are many statistical measures. Chapters 8, 9, and 10 will show you how to compute several of them. This chapter presents an overview, beginning with some basic information that is necessary to be able to use any statistical measures correctly.

Levels of Measurement

The term *level of measurement* refers to the classifications or units that result when a variable has been operationally defined. There are three levels of measurement with which you need to be familiar: nominal, ordinal, and interval data.

Nominal Variables

The "lowest" level of measurement, that is, the least precise, is the nominal level. A *nominal* variable simply places each case into one of several *unordered categories.* Examples would include an individual's racial/ethnic status (African American, white, Hispanic, Asian, Native American, or other), religious preference (Protestant, Catholic, Jewish, none, other), and vote for president (Clinton, Dole, Perot, other, not voting). Note that it would make no sense to describe such variables in quantitative terms. To speak of "more race," "less religion," or "more voting" from data on these measures would be silly. Nominal variables contain information on "what kind," not "how much."

Ordinal Variables

As the name implies, *ordinal* variables rank cases in relation to each other. This can take two forms. The first, *rank order*, puts the cases in exact order according to some characteristic. For example, we could rank states in order of population, with California being first, New York second, and so on. Note that these rank values do not carry as much information as the actual population figures on which they are based would. A state that is ranked tenth in population does not have twice as many people as the state ranked twentieth. Rank order is not much used in analysis for research purposes. In order to get an exact ranking, we usually would need numerical measures of the actual quantity of the variable. These would be *interval* values (discussed below), and it is preferable to treat such variables as interval. In the rest of this book any references to ordinal variables will mean *ordered categories*, the more common form of an ordinal variable.

With *ordered categories*, variables are put into categories—as are nominal variables—but the categories have an *inherent order*. This could be done by taking a variable for which numerical (interval) data are available and grouping the cases into categories. For example, states could be grouped by population into categories such as over 10 million, 1 million to 10 million, and under 1 million. Note that this sheds some of the information originally available. Ordinal category variables may also come directly from measures that do not have interval precision. For example, survey respondents might be ranked in social class by asking them if they consider themselves to be upper class, middle class, or working class.

Unlike nominal variables, ordinal variables, whether rank order or ordered categories, may be described in quantitative terms. It is proper to say that some cases in a data set have more education than others, even though education is measured only in terms of grade school, high school, or college.

In determining whether a set of categories may be considered as ordinal, it is important to remember that *all* categories must fit a pattern of high to low (or low to high) on the variable. The census categories of occupation (professional and managerial, clerical and sales, skilled manual, and unskilled manual) could be used as an ordinal measure of social status. However, the addition of the category of "farmers and farm laborers" would render the level as only nominal. The addition of residual categories such as "don't know," "not ascertained," or "other" will always cause the ordinal quality to be lost. In actual practice, this problem may be avoided if the researcher is willing to exclude all such cases from the analysis.

Interval Variables

The highest level of measurement is the interval level. An interval variable provides an exact number of whatever is being measured. This may be an actual count, for example, the total number of votes received by a candidate in a district or a person's annual income. Or it may be a standardized form, such as the percentage of the district voting Democratic or the average income of families in a state. This means that not only may interval variables be described in quantitative terms ("the higher the income, the lower the percentage Democratic"), but also exact comparisons may be made. For example, the difference between $5,000 and $10,000 of income is the same as the difference between $10,000 and $15,000. There is also another, similar level of measurement called a *ratio scale*. As the difference between interval and ratio levels is rarely important in social statistics, it will not be discussed here.

Box 6.1 provides a number of examples of variables and their level of measurement. Exercise A at the end of the chapter provides additional examples for you to test your understanding.

Rules for Using Levels of Measurement

These three levels of measurement are relatively simple concepts, though which level applies in some actual cases may be debatable. But the application is complicated by the fact that there are two

---

BOX 6.1   Examples of Level of Measurement

Highest

Interval level:
- Gross national product (in millions of U.S. dollars)
- Voter turnout (as percentage of voting age population)
- Percentage Catholic
- Years of education
- Crime rate (number of crimes per 100,000 population)

Ordinal:
- Seniority in the Senate (as of this writing, Senator Strom Thurmond is first, etc.)
- Level of economic development (developed, newly industrialized, less developed)
- Age (18–20, 21–39, 40–59, 60 and older)
- Opinion on defense spending (increase, keep at present level, decrease, eliminate entirely)
- Ideology (very conservative, somewhat conservative, middle of the road, somewhat liberal, very liberal)

Nominal:
- Region (Northeast, Midwest, South, West)
- Form of government (democracy, monarchy, military authoritarian, marxist, other)
- Source of political information (television, radio, newspapers, magazines, talking to others, none)
- Party preference (Republican, Democrat, independent, other, none)
- Opinion on gays in the military (allow, not allow, no opinion)

Lowest

---

rules that allow variables to be treated as other levels under certain circumstances.

Rule 1 is that a *variable may always be treated as a lower level of measurement*. This means that an interval variable may be treated as an ordinal or nominal variable, and an ordinal variable as a nominal variable. Thus, the percentage of a state's vote that went to the Democratic candidate, an interval variable, could be used to put the states into rank order from most Democratic to least Democratic. States could also be put into ordinal categories, such as over 60 percent Democratic, 50 percent to 60 percent Democratic, 40 percent to 49 percent Democratic, and so on. To treat these categories as nominal data, no changes are needed; one simply ignores the fact that they have an order.

In applying rule 1, it is critical to keep in mind that although you may go down in level of measurement from interval to ordinal to nominal, it is not permissible to go up, that is, to treat a nominal variable as ordinal or an ordinal variables as interval. There is one exception to that statement, and it constitutes the other rule.

Rule 2 is that a *dichotomy may be treated as any level of measurement.* A dichotomy is a variable that has two and only two possible values or categories. An example would be a person's gender (female or male), assuming that there were no cases in which that information was missing. A state could be classified as having a Republican or a Democratic governor. This would be a dichotomy as long as no state had an independent or third party governor. But if there are only two possible categories into which any cases can fall, the variable may be treated as interval, ordinal, or nominal, regardless of its substantive content. Thus, rule 2 might be expressed as "dichotomies are wild"—in the card-playing sense, of course.

In order to take advantage of rule 2, it is common for researchers to modify their data to create dichotomies. The motivation for this is that the statistics that can be used only for interval variables are more powerful than those for ordinal and nominal data. Hence, for example, the ethnicity of individuals might be condensed from the nominal set of categories of white, African American, Hispanic, Asian American, and other into the dichotomy of white and non-white. In political analysis it is common to collapse the regions of the United States into a Southern/Non-Southern dichotomy. Sophisticated multivariate analyses sometimes create what is called a *dummy* variable by using each category in a nominal variable, such as religious preference, to create new dichotomous variables—for example, Protestant/Non-Protestant, Catholic/Non-Catholic, and so on.

Box 6.2 provides some examples of the application of these two rules, as does Exercise B at the end of the chapter.

Why Levels of Measurement Are Important

The reason it is so important to be able to identify the level of measurement and correctly apply the rules is that each of the many statistics designed for data analysis makes assumptions about the variables' level of measurement. If you use an inappropriate statistic to evaluate your data, the results may be meaningless and lead you to draw erroneous conclusions. This is something to bear in mind when using computers in statistical analysis. The computer programs we use to calculate statistical values do not know what the content of your variables is and therefore cannot determine what statistics should be used. Since it is common to enter all kinds of data as numbers, the computer will readily treat any variable as interval data, even though the numbers may represent arbitrary codes for nominal categories. A variable such as region may be coded 1 for Northeast, 2 for Midwest, 3 for South, and 4 for West. To compute the "average region" would be senseless, but a statistical program will do it if you request it.

Therefore, always be aware of the level of measurement of your variables and of what levels the two rules will allow you to treat them as. As noted earlier, you may choose to modify a variable, such as by collapsing it into a dichotomy, to take advantage of rule 2. Most computer programs can do this for you automatically.

What Is a Statistic?

As noted at the start of this chapter, in social science research we are often faced with the task of looking at a large collection of observations and trying to see what patterns are present. Such a task would be difficult and in many cases impossible if we did not have statistics to assist us. A *statistic* may be defined as *a numerical measure that summarizes some characteristic of a larger body of data.* That is why statistics are useful. They can reduce very large amounts of information, such as the census of the United States, to single numbers that convey information we need.

Statistics are found in everyday life, and everyone uses them. The most common statistic is the total, such as the total population of a nation or the total amount of money in one's pocket. Another

BOX 6.2   Rules for Using Level of Measurement and Examples of Their Application

Rule 1: "Down, But Not Up": A variable may always be treated as a *lower* level of measurement (i.e., interval may be treated as ordinal, or nominal and ordinal may be treated as a nominal. But never treat a variable as a higher level.

Rule 2: "Dichotomies Are Wild": A dichotomy—a variable with only two possible values—may be treated as any level of measurement.

Examples:

Percentage of a nation's budget spent on defense: This is an interval variable, so it could also be treated as ordinal or nominal (rule 1).

Party competition in a state (highly competitive, less competitive, one party): This is an ordinal variable, so it could also be treated as nominal (rule 1).

NATO membership (member, nonmember): This is a dichotomy, so it could be treated as nominal, ordinal, or interval (rule 2).

Form of municipal government (strong mayor, council-manager, commission, other): This is a nominal variable and not a dichotomy, so it could only be treated as nominal.

Level of education, **variation 1** (grade school, some high school, high school graduate, some college, college graduate): This is ordinal, so it could also be treated as nominal (rule 1).

Level of education, **variation 2** (grade school, some high school, high school graduate, some college, college graduate, trade school, still in school, unknown): This is a nominal variable because the addition of any of the last three categories deprives it of its otherwise ordinal quality. Therefore, it can be treated only as nominal.

continues

---

continued

Population density (number of people per square mile): This is an interval variable, so it could be treated as nominal and ordinal as well (rule 1).

Legislator's vote on bill (yea, nay): This is a dichotomy, so it may be treated as nominal, ordinal, or interval (rule 2).

---

common statistic is the *proportion*, which can be expressed as a decimal, a fraction, or a percentage. *Rates* are also a familiar statistic, such as miles per gallon for automobile fuel consumption. The *average*, the term most people use for the *arithmetic mean*, is a well-known statistic. Viewed in this way, the subject of statistics is not an exotic undertaking, but simply an extension of a tool you have been using for years. Since scientific research goes beyond simple description and attempts to analyze relationships and test hypotheses, you will need some new tools in your toolbox.

Univariate Statistics

All of the examples of everyday statistics cited above are *univariate*, that is, they describe characteristics of one variable at a time. Since most readers already have some knowledge of them and since scientific research is usually concerned with multivariate questions, the discussion here will be brief.

Measures of Central Tendency

The most familiar univariate statistics are measures of central tendency—or, as they are commonly called, averages. There is a measure for each level of measurement. Each one is way of describing what the "typical" case in a set looks like on some variable.

The best known is the *mean,* or arithmetic average, which can be computed only for interval data. The mean is computed by adding up all of the individual values and dividing by the number of cases.

A similar measure is the *median,* or "middle" value in a distribution: Half of the cases have higher values and half have lower values. Technically, a median can be determined from ordinal data, but it is usually computed for interval values. Suppose we have a very small town of five families and their incomes are $2,000, $2,000, $3,000, $4,000, and $89,000. The mean family income for this town would be $20,000, but the median would be only $3,000. In cases such as this, with highly *skewed* distributions (i.e., where there are some extreme cases, which can greatly affect the mean), the median is often considered to be a better measure of central tendency. In this example, the median income of $3,000 better describes the typical family than the mean of $20,000. But it should be remembered that the mean actually includes more information than the median.

A measure of central tendency that can be applied even to nominal data is the mode, which is simply the most frequently occurring value or category. In the example above, the mode would be $2,000. Modes are not very useful for interval data, especially when the values have a large potential range. Modes are sometimes useful for describing ordinal category or nominal data. For example, the modal ethnic category in the U.S. is white, because more people fall into that category than any other.

Measures of Dispersion

Another characteristic of a set of observations is the extent to which they are *dispersed*, that is, how closely or widely cases are separated on a variable. Measures of dispersion can be computed only for interval data. We could have two distributions of observations with the same mean and median that are very different from one another. For example, to take two more very small towns, one might have five families with incomes of $2,000, $2,000, $20,000, $38,000, and $38,000, and the other five families with incomes of $18,000, $19,000, $20,000, $38,000, and $38,000. In both communities the mean and the median income is $20,000. But in the first community, income is dispersed over a wide range, whereas in the second the incomes are more similar to one another.

The simplest measure of dispersion is the *range*, which is simply the difference between the highest and the lowest values. In the first town the range is $36,000, and in the second it is $4,000. The range is not a very useful measure, however, because it is so easily affected by the presence of even one extreme case. There are more sophisticated versions such as the *quartile range*, which is half the difference between the values of the cases that rank one-fourth and three-fourths of the way between the highest and lowest scores. But even this sort of measure is not as precise as one might wish.

The most common measure of dispersion is the *standard deviation*, which is based on a summation of the difference of each case from the mean. Although this is sometimes useful as a measure in itself, it is most commonly used in performing certain tests of statistical significance.

The Concept of Relationship

As should be clear from earlier chapters, scientific research is usually concerned with *multivariate* questions—the relationship between two or more variables. The concept of relationships between variables was introduced earlier, but now we will see what such relationships look like. In order to do this, we must first understand how data can be assembled to view possible relationships.

Contingency Tables

The way data on two nominal or ordinal category variables are customarily presented is by use of a cross-tabulation, or *contingency table*. This is a table showing the frequencies of each combination of categories on the two variables. Constructing one is simply a process of counting up how many cases fall into each combination. Box 6.3A shows a set of "raw" data and the resulting contingency table. In this example, one would first go through the data and count up how many males voted Republican, then how many females, and so on.

Contingency tables are often presented in terms of percentages. This can be done in several ways; the percentages might add up to 100 for each column, for each row, or for the entire table. However, it is usually clearest for the reader if the following conventions are followed: (1) Let the independent variable define the columns and the dependent variable define the rows. (2) Compute column percentages by dividing the frequency of each cell by the total for that column. (If this is done, the percentages for each column will add up to 100.) Box 6.3B shows a contingency table with raw frequencies and their percentages in proper form. Note that it is desirable to include the N, which is the number of cases on which each set of percentages is based. The variables and categories should also be clearly labeled.

BOX 6.3   The Contingency Table

A. Constructing the Table

Raw Data

GENDER	VOTE
M	R
F	R
M	R
F	D
M	D
F	D
M	R
F	R
F	D
M	D

Contingency Table

	GENDER	
	Male	Female
VOTE Republican:	3	2
Democratic:	2	3

B. Expressing the Table in Terms of Percentages

RAW FREQUENCIES

	GENDER	
	Male	Female
VOTE		
Republican:	557	429
Democratic:	439	586

PERCENTAGES

	GENDER	
	Male	Female
VOTE		
Republican:	56 %	42 %
Democratic:	44	58
	100 %	100 %
	N=996	N=1,005

Scattergrams

To show interval data in a contingency table would not make much sense, as there would have to be rows and columns for each of the individual values of the variables, and most cells would have a frequency of 1 or 0. Instead, relationships between two interval variables are shown in a *scattergram* (also called a scatterplot). Box 6.4 gives an example of a small set of interval data and the resulting scattergram. Note that the *horizontal axis is always used for the in-*

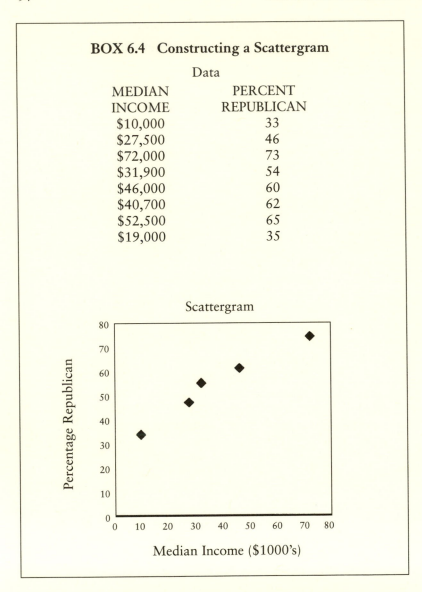

BOX 6.4   **Constructing a Scattergram**

Data

MEDIAN INCOME	PERCENT REPUBLICAN
$10,000	33
$27,500	46
$72,000	73
$31,900	54
$46,000	60
$40,700	62
$52,500	65
$19,000	35

Scattergram

dependent variable and the vertical axis for the dependent variable. To construct this scattergram, one would first go across the horizontal axis to the value of the independent variable—income in this case—and then straight up to the height of the dependent variable—percent Republican—and at that intersection place a dot indicating the position of the case. When this is done for all cases, the result is a scattergram. (In some cases, numbers or letters identifying the cases are used instead of dots.)

What Does a Relationship Look Like?

To say that there is a relationship between two variables implies that the cases are not distributed randomly, but rather that there is some *identifiable pattern*. With ordinal or interval data this can be described in quantitative terms; for example, the more education one has, the higher one's income tends to be. Relationships between nominal variables may be described in terms of contrast between categories, for example, that Catholics are more likely to be Democrats than are Protestants. But the different types of possible relationships can best be illustrated with contingency tables and scattergrams.

Box 6.5 attempts to do this by showing what contingency tables and scattergrams would look like if there were absolutely no relationship between two variables as compared with a "perfect" relationship, which can take either a positive or negative form with ordinal and interval variables. Consider part A for nominal variables. Where there is no relationship, the percentage columns in the contingency table are exactly the same. As one moves across a row, the figures do not change. It makes no difference in this hypothetical data set whether a person is Protestant, Catholic, or Jewish; 37 percent of each religion is Republican. Religion would be of no value in predicting a person's party affiliation. On the other hand, the example of a perfect relationship shows a different situation entirely. All Protestants are Republican, all Catholics are Democratic, and all Jews are independent. This means that we could perfectly predict a person's party identification by knowing his or her religion.

The same is true of the examples for ordinal variables in part B of Box 6.5. The no-relationship example shows that each educational group has exactly the same income distribution. But in the example of a perfect positive relationship, all individuals who went to college have a high income, those who went to high school all have a medium income, and those who went only to grade school all have a low income. Therefore, for this hypothetical data set, we can say that the more education a person has, the higher his or her income, and one variable could perfectly predict the other. In the

BOX 6.5   Examples of No Relationship and Perfect Relationships

A. *Nominal Variables*

		No Relationship RELIGION		
		Prot	*Cath*	*Jew*
PARTY	Rep	37%	37%	37%
ID	Ind	39	39	39
	Dem	24	24	24
		100%	100%	100%

Correlation = 0.00

		Perfect Relationship RELIGION		
		Prot	*Cath*	*Jew*
PARTY	Rep	100%	0%	0%
ID	Ind	0	0	100
	Dem	0	100	0
		100%	100%	100%

Correlation = 1.00

B. *Ordinal Variables*

Perfect Relationships

	No Relationship EDUCATION				Positive EDUCATION				Negative EDUCATION		
INCOME	*Col*	*HS*	*GS*		*Col*	*HS*	*GS*		*Col*	*HS*	*GS*
Hi	30%	30%	30%	Hi	100%	0%	0%	Hi	0%	0%	100%
Med	42	42	42	Med	0	100	0	Med	0	100	0
Low	28	28	28	Low	0	0	100	Low	100	0	0
	100%	100%	100%		100%	100%	100%		100%	100%	100%

Correlation = 0.00   Correlation = +1.00   Correlation = −1.00

C. *Interval Variables*

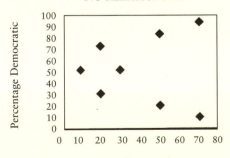

continues

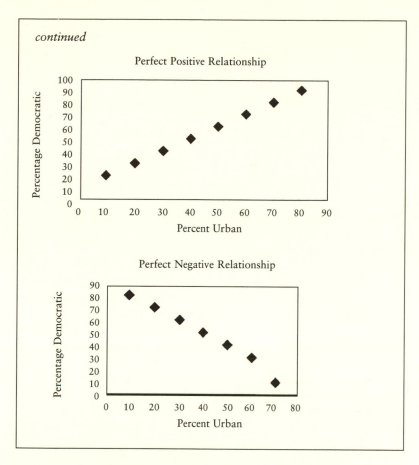

example of a negative relationship, the predictability is again perfect, but in the opposite direction. In this unlikely example, all college people have low incomes and all those who went only to grade
school have high incomes.

In part C of Box 6.5, scattergrams are presented for a pair of interval variables. In the no-relationship example, the cases are randomly distributed with no pattern. In the example of a perfect positive relationship, all the cases fall on a straight line, so it is clear
that the more urban an area, the higher the Democratic percentage
of the vote. This would allow us to compute the equation for that
straight line and therefore predict the vote for any case from its urbanization score (how to do this will be covered in Chapter 9). The
same is true in the negative relationship example, except that the

line slopes downward, indicating that the more urban an area, the less Democratic its voting pattern.

Multivariate Statistics

Three characteristics of a relationship between variables can be summarized by statistics: *strength, direction,* and *significance.* It is critical to understand the difference between them.

Strength of a Relationship

The strength of a relationship is a measure of where the relationship falls between no relationship and a perfect relationship. It can also be thought of as a relative measure of how good a predictor the independent variable is of the dependent variable.

There are many statistics designed to measure *strength of association.* These are commonly called *correlations.* (A number of them are summarized below in Table 6.1, and several are presented in detail in Chapters 8, 9, and 10.) Although these statistics are designed for different combinations of levels of measurement and differ in their sensitivity to various aspects of the distribution of the variables, they all have two things in common. First, if there is absolutely no relationship between the variables, they will have a value of zero. (However, some define "no relationship" a little differently than others.) Second, if there is a "perfect" relationship, all will have a value of one, though it might be either plus one or minus one, depending on the direction of the relationship, as discussed below. Thus, for example, the "no relationship" tables and graph in each part of Box 6.5 all would have a correlation of exactly zero, using any of the many measures of strength of association. The "perfect relationship" tables and graphs would each have a correlation value of plus one or minus one, depending on whether the relationship is in a positive or negative direction.

Direction of a Relationship

The *direction* of a relationship is a simple concept. It answers the question of what happens to the dependent variable as the independent variable increases. If the dependent variable also increases, then the relationship is said to be positive. If the dependent variable decreases, the relationship is negative.

Direction in this sense applies only to ordinal or interval variables. A purely nominal variable, such as an individual's religious preference or ethnicity, cannot be said to increase or decrease. The direction of relationships as indicated by statistics computed on ordinal category data is completely dependent on the order of the columns and rows. In the example in part B of Box 6.5, reversing the order of the columns on education or the rows on income (but not both) would reverse the plus or minus sign for any correlation. That is one reason why it is always important to look closely at the contingency table, preferably one in terms of percentages, before drawing conclusions about relations between categorized variables.

Significance of a Relationship

The term *significance* has a special meaning in statistics. Significance refers to the *probability that a relationship between variables could have occurred by chance in a random sample if there were no relationship between them in the population from which the sample was drawn.* Recall from the discussion of survey sampling in Chapter 5 that even properly taken samples are a matter of chance. For that reason, there is always a confidence interval around an estimate made from a sample. The same idea applies to relationships between variables in sample data, though it is expressed differently.

The probability of a relationship occurring by chance is, essentially, the probability that one might make a mistake by drawing the conclusion that the relationship observed in the sample is true of the larger population. Therefore, *the smaller that probability, the more significant the relationship.* In most social science research, *if the probability is .05 or less, then the relationship is said to be significant.* There are quite a number of significance tests, some of which are listed below in Table 6.1 and several of which are covered in detail in Chapters 8, 9, and 10. But the *.05 level of significance applies to all significance tests.* This, incidentally, is the same thing as the 95 percent level of confidence cited in the discussion of survey sampling in Chapter 5.

It is important to remember that *significance tests should be used only if the data are from a random sample.* If the data are from a sample that has not been selected by one of the appropriate methods described in Chapter 5, then significance tests have no validity. But what if the data are not from a sample at all, but constitute a whole population, such as all fifty U.S. states or all 100 Senators?

Then significance tests, while not necessarily inaccurate, are unnecessary. If there is even a very weak correlation between two characteristics of the fifty states, then we can be sure that it exists, though it may not be of any importance.

As will become clear when you learn how to conduct some significance tests in later chapters, the significance of a relationship is determined by two factors: the *strength of the correlation* and the *sample size*. The stronger the correlation between two variables, the less the probability that it was a chance occurrence and, therefore, the more significant it will be. But it also depends on how large the sample is. The same degree of strength might be significant in a large sample, but not achieve significance in a small sample. It is important to keep this in mind when interpreting data, whether in analyzing your own or reading the results of another person's research. In large samples, such as surveys with over 1,000 cases, even very weak relationships may be "statistically significant," even though they are of little substantive importance.

With all of this background, we can now take a look at Table 6.1, which summarizes a number of (but certainly not all) the statistics designed to evaluate relationships. All of these are *bivariate* statistics—they evaluate relationships between two variables. There are also statistics that deal with the relationship between three or more variables, but these are all extensions of Pearson's r, so the same assumptions and interpretations apply. These statistics are discussed in Chapter 10.

Table 6.1 can be useful when reading the results of someone else's research and encountering an unfamiliar statistic. It can also be useful when analyzing data using a computer program that offers a wide choice of possible statistics. But it is highly inadvisable to use a statistic with which one is not familiar. There are many details and variations that a simple summary like Table 6.1 cannot cover.

Exercises

Exercise A

For each of the following variables, identify the level of measurement (nominal, ordinal, or interval).

1. Opinion on legality of abortion (always, only under certain circumstances, never).

TABLE 6.1   Common Bivariate Statistics

Level of Measurement	Measures of Association	Range	Tests of Significance
Two nominal variables			
	*Lambda	0 to+1.0	*Chi²
	*Phi	0 to+1.0	
	Cramer's V	0 to+1.0	
	Tau$_B$	0 to+1.0	
The ordinal variables	*Gamma	-1.0 to +1.0	*Chi²
	Kendall's Tau$_B$	-1.0 to +1.0	
	Kendall's Tau$_C$	-1.0 to +1.0	
Two interval variables	*Pearson's r	-1.0 to +1.0	*F-test
One nominal variable and one interval variable	Eta	0 to+1.0	F-test
			t-test
			Difference of Means

*Statistics covered in detail in Chapters 7, 8, and 9.

2. Outcome of a congressional vote on a bill (pass, fail).
3. Number of irregular executive transfers in a nation since 1980.
4. Previous colonial power (Britain, France, Spain, other, none).
5. Size of largest city (Over 1 million, 100,000 to 1 million, less than 100,000).

Exercise B

For the examples in Exercise A, apply rules 1 and 2 and identify *all* of the levels of measurement the variable could be considered as, including the original level.

Exercise C

Below are data on religion and turnout for fifteen people. For these
data:

1. Construct a contingency table showing the frequencies.
2. Present the table in terms of percentages, using proper form.
3. Draw a conclusion about the relationship between religion
   and turnout for these individuals.

Religion	Turnout	Religion	Turnout	Religion	Turnout
P	V	J	V	C	V
C	V	C	N	P	N
J	V	C	V	J	V
P	N	P	V	C	N
C	V	P	V	P	N

Codes for Variables: Religion: P = Protestant, C = Catholic, J = Jewish
Turnout: V = Voter, N = Nonvoter

Suggested Answers to Exercises

Exercise A

1. Ordinal
2. Nominal
3. Interval
4. Nominal
5. Ordinal

Exercise B

1. Ordinal, nominal (rule 1)
2. Interval, ordinal, nominal (rule 2)
3. Interval, ordinal, nominal (rule 1)
4. Nominal (neither rule applies)
5. Ordinal, nominal (rule 1)

Exercise C

1.

Frequency table			
	Religion		
	Prot	Cath	Jew
Turnout: Voter	3	4	3
Nonvoter	3	2	0

2.

Percentage table			
	Religion		
	Prot	Cath	Jew
Turnout: Voter	50%	67%	100%
Nonvoter	50	33	0
	100%	100%	100%

3. There is a relationship between religion and turnout in that Catholics have higher turnout than Protestants, and Jews have the highest.

7

Graphic Display
of Data

Popular media such as newspapers and magazines frequently use graphics to report the distribution of results in some form of picture—a chart or graph instead of (or in addition to) reporting the relevant numbers. The purpose of these graphic displays is primarily to convey important characteristics more effectively than a verbal description or table of numbers would be able to do. The use of graphics has increased markedly in the past decade, primarily because of the ease of constructing and printing graphs and charts with widely available computer programs.

This chapter has two purposes. The first is to illustrate how to construct several common types of graphics while avoiding many common mistakes. The second is to explain how to interpret graphics you might encounter in your reading—and not be misled when others make the common mistakes.

Construction of graphics may seem simple to do with a computer, but doing it correctly involves understanding concepts covered earlier in this book, including the distinction between independent and dependent variables and the three levels of measurement discussed in Chapter 6. Since many people who put graphics into their articles, reports, and papers are not familiar with these concepts, the graphics that result are frequently meaningless or even misleading. Graphic displays of data can be very useful, both for conveying information to the reader and for researchers to better understand their data. (The scattergram described in Chapter 6 is particularly useful for this latter function.) But from the standpoint of *scientific research*, two disclaimers are in order. First, graphics of the type presented in this chapter can almost never present information as complete as a numerical table can—and generally they present much less. Second, reports of scientific research such as those found in scholarly journals generally do not use these simple graphics. This chapter provides only a limited introduction to the topic. (A brief yet comprehensive treatment of the subject can be found in Wallgren et al. 1996.)

Graphics for Univariate Distributions

The simplest use of graphics is to display the distribution of cases on a single variable such as the proportion of people who belong to different religions. Typically what is being graphed is a nominal or ordinal category variable or a variable that has been made into one, such as by placing individuals' incomes into different ranges. Such variables can be visually displayed in several ways, such as pie charts and bar charts.

Pie Charts

Pie charts are circles that are divided into segments representing different categories, the relative size of the segment being proportional to the frequency of the category. Figure 7.1 is an example (all of the figures in this chapter were produced by Microsoft Excel). Often different colors or shadings are used to distinguish the categories.

Although pie charts are frequently found in newspapers, magazines, and similar popular media, they are really not very useful. Most readers have trouble making a precise comparison of the size of circular wedges. For this reason, it is common to include the exact numbers or percentages in the pie chart—but this is exactly the same information that would be presented in a simple numerical table. A number of authorities on graphic presentation advise against using pie charts (e.g., Tufte 1983, 178).

Bar Charts

A more useful method of displaying category frequencies is the bar chart. Here the relative frequency of each category is represented by

FIGURE 7.1   Popular vote for president, 1996

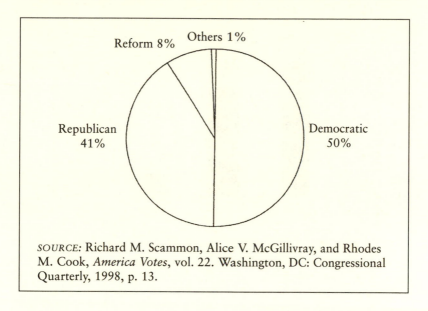

Reform 8%   Others 1%

Republican
41%

Democratic
50%

SOURCE: Richard M. Scammon, Alice V. McGillivray, and Rhodes
M. Cook, *America Votes*, vol. 22. Washington, DC: Congressional
Quarterly, 1998, p. 13.

the height of a bar. The bars are usually vertical, but may be horizontal. Bar charts are somewhat superior to pie charts in that most
people can more easily compare the simple lengths of bars or lines
than the relative sizes of segments of a circle, but again the information communicated is less precise than would be a simple reporting of the actual frequencies, especially in terms of percentages.
Therefore, the bar chart, too, may well include the precise numbers.
If a bar chart does not include the precise frequencies, then it should
present a scale on the vertical axis, as was done in Figure 7.2. Unfortunately, such charts in popular media often fail to do this.

Graphics for Multivariate Relationships

There are a number of ways the relationship between two or more
variables can be shown graphically. One is to use the bar chart.
Here the different bars represent different categories of the independent variable, and their heights represent the dependent variable. Hence, the independent variable must be a nominal or ordinal category variable, and the dependent variable either
frequencies—whether actual numbers or percentages—or an inter-

FIGURE 7.2   Popular vote for president, 1996

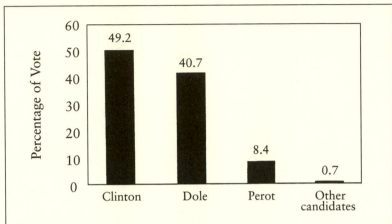

SOURCE: Richard M. Scammon, Alice V. McGillivray, and Rhodes M. Cook, *America Votes*, vol. 22. Washington, DC: Congressional Quarterly, 1998, p. 13.

val variable. Figure 7.3 is an example. As with the univariate bar chart, showing the exact numerical value of the height of the bar, or at least including a scale, is desirable but unfortunately is not always done.

Bar charts can also be used to illustrate the relationship between three variables. These charts use bars whose height represents the frequency (or interval value) of the dependent variable for each combination of categories of the independent and control variables. (It does not matter which variable is the independent and which is the control variable.) Such charts could be constructed from the results of *controlling using contingency tables*, which is discussed in Chapter 10. This approach could be extended to any number of independent and/or control variables, but the results would be very hard for the reader to interpret. Figure 7.4 is an example of a chart showing the effects of controlling.

Line Graphs

Another method of illustrating the relationship between an interval dependent variable and an ordinal category independent variable is

FIGURE 7.3   Reported voter turnout, by ethnicity, 1996

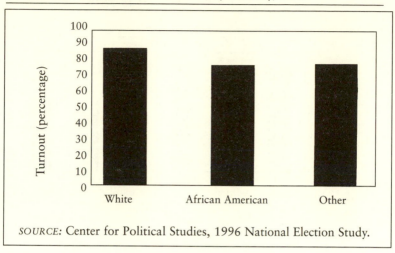

SOURCE: Center for Political Studies, 1996 National Election Study.

the line graph. Essentially, a line graph is the same as a bar chart, except that instead of using a bar to represent the value of the dependent variable, a single point takes the place of the top of each bar, and then the points are connected with a line. Although line graphs can be used where the independent variable categories are nominal (such as ethnic groups), it is best reserved for instances where the independent variable is ordinal. The line graph is preferable to the bar chart when there are so many categories of the independent variable that a bar chart would be confusing. Therefore, line graphs often are used to display data over a lengthy time period. Figure 7.5 is an example of a line graph. Note that line graphs should *not be confused with scattergrams* (Chapter 6) and the line connecting the points in a line graph should *never be confused with the regression line* (Chapter 8).

How Not to Lie with Graphics

How to Lie with Statistics (Huff 1954) is a famous book first published nearly half a century ago but still available. Its purpose is to show how the popular media—particularly advertising—frequently mislead the reader through their presentation of quantitative data, and frequently involving graphics. The kinds of problems Huff cited, whether committed intentionally or by mistake, are all the

FIGURE 7.4   Reported voter turnout, by ethnicity and education, 1996

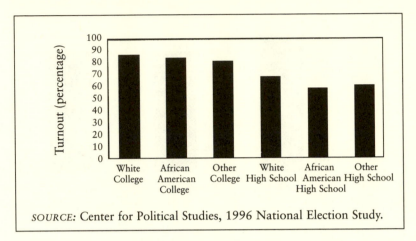

SOURCE: Center for Political Studies, 1996 National Election Study.

more common today. (A recent attempt to make the same point can be found in Almer 2000.) It is important to be aware of these errors, both to avoid making them oneself and to prevent being misled when looking at the work of others.

The Missing Zero Point

Perhaps the most frequent problem with bar charts and line graphs is that the vertical axis either does not go down to zero or part of the axis is omitted. The effect of this is to exaggerate the contrast between different categories of the independent variable. For example, if we were to draw a graph or chart of the budget of some government agency over several years, and the budget increased from $100 million to $105 million, then a correctly rendered graphic would show what it should—that spending increased only very slightly. However, if we were to place the horizontal line that showed the years not at the zero dollars point on the vertical axis but at the $95 million level, then the graph would at first sight give the impression that spending had doubled over this period. If we omitted any specific numbers or scales, the graph would be completely misleading. Including the numbers would make the graphic technically correct, but it still might mislead the casual reader. Figures 7.6A and 7.6B show an example of how such a graphic should and should not be constructed.

FIGURE 7.5   Turnout of voting-age population in presidential elections, 1960–1996

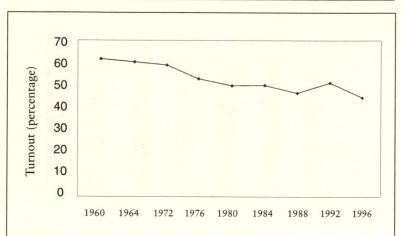

SOURCE: Paul R. Abramson, John H. Aldrich, and David W. Rhode, *Change and Continuity in the 1996 and 1998 Elections.* Washington, DC: CQ Press, 1999, p. 69.

Scales and Axes

Line graphs can also be misleading because of problems with how the horizontal and vertical axes are defined. Assigning the independent and dependent variables to the wrong axes can be a major problem. When the independent variable is erroneously shown on the vertical axis and the dependent variable is erroneously shown on the horizontal axis, the relationship between the two variables may appear completely the opposite of what it really is. Relationships also may be distorted if the range of possible values for one variable is shown in a much shorter length than that used for the other variable.

Misleading Pictorials

Pictorials are graphics similar to bar charts, except that rather than simple bars whose length represents the value of a variable, a picture of some object is used, such as a sack of grain, a dollar sign, or a person. Pictorials are never used in scientific reporting, but they

FIGURE 7.6A   U.S. per pupil spending on education, 1990–1996—
correctly presented

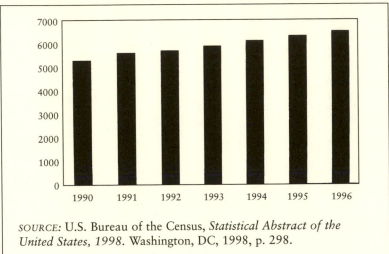

SOURCE: U.S. Bureau of the Census, *Statistical Abstract of the
United States, 1998*. Washington, DC, 1998, p. 298.

are found in popular media and advertising. They are particularly
likely to be misleading because the picture size is proportional to
the variable's value not only in height but also in width, and sometimes in depth. Thus if one category of the variable has a value
twice as high as another, its picture would give the impression that
the value was four (or even eight) times as great. And since these
pictorials are sometimes presented with no specific values or scales
attached, the reader would have no way of detecting the misrepre-
sentation.

The Need for Standardization

The need for standardization was demonstrated in the discussion
of operational definitions in Chapter 2. Whenever we are presenting data on aggregates, such as cities or states, the measure is likely
to be meaningful only if it is presented in some way that is standardized, usually to population, such as percentages or per capita
figures. Since most graphics present aggregate data, this is particularly important. A bar graph showing the total number of crimes
committed in different states might give the impression that Cali-

FIGURE 7.6B   U.S. per pupil spending on education, 1990–1996—
incorrectly presented

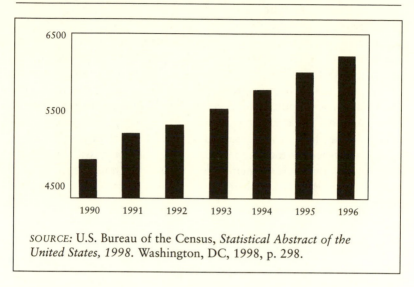

SOURCE: U.S. Bureau of the Census, *Statistical Abstract of the United States, 1998.* Washington, DC, 1998, p. 298.

fornia and New York are far more dangerous places to live than smaller states, whereas the same chart based on crime rates (i.e., crimes per 100,000 population) would show much less difference, and small states would not always have the lowest rates.

The same principle holds when our unit of analysis is time (i.e., comparing different time periods), because population sizes change. But when dealing with variables measured in dollars or any other unit of currency, we also need to control for inflation. A graphic showing the incomes of any U.S. population group in different years will generally show a significant increase over time, but that would be largely the result of decreases in the value of the dollar every year for many decades. Therefore, responsible graphics (or verbal presentations of the same information) always present these figures in terms of *constant dollars,* that is, the amounts are adjusted for inflation.

Principles for Good Graphics

Aside from avoiding the errors noted above (it is assumed that you would not want to mislead anyone), what are the rules for using graphic displays correctly and effectively?

Keep It Simple

The purpose of a graphic is to convey certain characteristics of data to the reader more effectively, and this is best done by making the graphic as simple as possible. Large numbers of categories in pie or bar charts are apt to be confusing. If a large number of categories are necessary for full presentation of the data, then a table is a better choice than a chart or graph. Extensive verbal explanations in the body of a graphic should be avoided, as should unnecessary artwork, fancy borders, and the like. If you are printing a graphic such as a pie chart or a segmented bar chart where categories must be distinguished by their appearance and it is not possible to print them in different colors, then different shadings must be used. But keep the shadings as simple as possible, avoiding the use of cross-hatching.

Verbal Aspects of Graphics

Although unnecessary wording within a graphic should be avoided, some use of words is essential to any chart or graph. Within the graphic, it is essential that the variables be clearly labeled, including the units in which they are measured. Every graphic should have a title above it specifying what the graph is, again including the variables. Finally, if the data are not generated from the research you are presenting but are from another source, that source should be identified, usually on a line below the graphic. The same rules, incidentally, also apply to any numerical tables you present.

Describing the Graphic in the Text

Too often graphics are thrown into a paper with little or no discussion in the text. There should always be a description of the table, including the conclusion that the author wishes the reader to draw. In some circles it is a maxim that every table, chart, or graph that appears in a scientific report ought to have at least a page of discussion. Although a page may be more than is always necessary, certainly a paragraph is needed. If there is nothing to be said about a graphic, then one would have to question whether it is really worth including.

If you have more than one graphic, it should be labeled in its title (e.g., Figure 1) and then specific reference can be made in the text to that figure so that the reader will be looking at the appropriate picture. Again, these comments apply to tables as well as to graphics.

Exercises

Exercise A

Below is a table showing the frequency of poverty in different ethnic groups in the United States for several years. Design and produce two appropriate graphics (either by hand or on a computer) illustrating (1) the relative frequency of poverty in ethnic groups in 1996, and (2) the change in the frequency of poverty for the whole population ("All Races") from 1976 to 1996. For each graphic, write a verbal description of what appears to be happening.

Persons Below Poverty Level 1976–1996 (percentages)				
	All Races	White	Black	Hispanic
1976	11.8	9.1	31.1	26.9
1986	13.6	11.0	31.4	29.0
1996	13.7	11.2	28.4	29.4

SOURCE: U.S. Bureau of the Census, *Statistical Abstract of the United States, 1998*. Washington, DC, 1998, table 756.

Exercise B

Find an example of one of the types of graphics described in this chapter from a newspaper or magazine. Evaluate this graphic—is it misleading in any way? Are there any details or information that should have been included? Was there an adequate discussion in the accompanying text (if any)? Could you suggest a better type of graphic to present this information?

Suggested Answers to Exercise A

FIGURE 7.7   Percentage of persons below poverty level, by ethnic
status, 1996

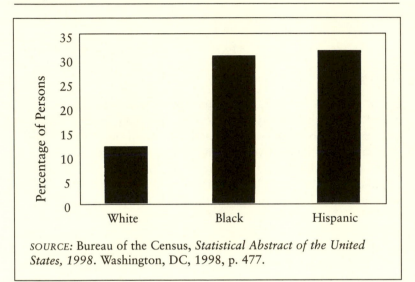

SOURCE: Bureau of the Census, *Statistical Abstract of the United States, 1998.* Washington, DC, 1998, p. 477.

FIGURE 7.8   Percentage of persons below poverty level, 1976–1996

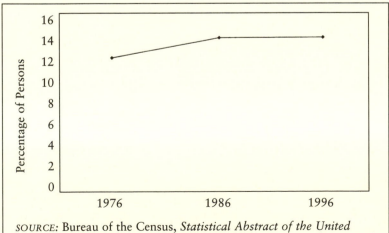

SOURCE: Bureau of the Census, *Statistical Abstract of the United States, 1998.* Washington, DC, 1998, p. 477.

8

Nominal and Ordinal Statistics

This chapter presents detailed explanations of several measures of strength of association (correlations) and one test of significance appropriate for contingency tables with nominal and ordinal variables. Students sometimes wonder whether it is practical to learn how actually to compute such measures; after all, computer programs are almost always used for the task. There are two reasons why it is useful to have some familiarity with methods of computation. One is that you may occasionally find yourself looking at a simple frequency table for which it might be quicker simply to compute a statistic by hand than to enter the data into a computer. The more important reason, however, is that knowledge of how a statistic is defined and computed provides a deeper understanding of its meaning, which is valuable in understanding how to apply and interpret it correctly.

Correlations for Nominal Variables

Lambda (λ) is a correlational statistic that measures the *strength of association* between *two nominal variables*. Therefore, it may be used for any contingency table, according to rule 1 for the use of levels of measurement. The range of possible values for lambda is from 0 to +1, that is, from no relationship to a perfect relationship. Therefore, a value of lambda that results in a negative number or a number greater than 1 is a result of an error in computation.

Lambda measures *proportional reduction of error*; that is, it measures how much better one can predict the value of each case on the dependent variable if one knows the value of the independent variable. The formula for lambda is a simple one:

$$\text{Lambda} = \frac{b-a}{b}$$

where b is the number of errors one would make in predicting the value of each case on the dependent variable if one did not know the value of the independent variables, and a is the number of errors one would make when the value of the independent variable *is* known.

This is a simple idea, but it can be a little tricky at first. Consider the contingency table below. Since we will need the marginal row totals, they are included with the table.

		RELIGION			
		Prot	Cath	Jew	(Total)
VOTE	Clinton	39	30	7	(76)
	Dole	47	16	2	(65)
	Perot	10	4	1	(15)

Suppose we had a group of 156 people and knew nothing about them except the overall distribution of their votes (the row totals) from the table above. If we had to guess how any given individual voted, it would be best to guess that he or she voted for Clinton. We would be correct on the 76 who did vote for Clinton, but wrong on the 65 who voted for Dole and the 15 who voted for Perot; this would be a total of 80 errors, which is therefore the value of b. But then if we take account of the independent variable, religion, and look within each column of the table, we can make another set of predictions using the same method as before. We would predict that each Protestant voted for Dole, as that is the best guess, but we would be wrong on the 39 Protestants who voted for Clinton and the 10 Protestants who voted for Perot. We would predict that all Catholics voted for Clinton, but would make errors on the 16 Catholic Dole voters and the 4 Perot voters. Similarly, we would predict that all Jews voted for Clinton, but be wrong on the 2 who voted for Dole and the 1 who voted for Perot.

Adding up all of these errors made within the religious categories (39 + 10 + 16 + 4 + 2 + 1), we arrive at a total of 72, which is the value of a. We can then use the formula to compute lambda:

$$\text{Lambda} = \frac{b-a}{b} = \frac{80-72}{80} = \frac{8}{80} = .10$$

The value of .1 shows that there is some relationship. Knowing a person's religion improved our prediction by 10 percent. This is a relatively weak relationship. But note that in comparison to some other correlations (particularly gamma, discussed below), values of lambda tend to be low.

Certain other features of lambda should be kept in mind. First of all, lambda sometimes has a value of zero even though there is a relationship between the variables. Consider the following table:

		GENDER	
		Male	Female
VOTE	Democratic	51	95
	Republican	49	5

If you were to compute lambda (you might try this for practice), the value would prove to be 0. The reason is that the largest number of voters in each gender category voted Democratic, even though it was to a very different degree. Whenever all categories of the independent variable have their greatest frequency in the same category of the dependent variable, lambda will be zero.

Second, *lambda is asymmetric*, that is, it makes a difference which variable is considered the independent and which the dependent variable. For instance, if we used the data from the first example to try to predict a person's religion from his or her vote, we would find that the value of lambda was 0. This is another reason one should always set up a contingency table with the independent variable defining the columns and the dependent variable defining the rows.

Third, *lambda must be computed from a table with "raw" frequencies*, not from a table expressed in percentages. This is because a table expressed in terms of column percentages will weight each column equally, even though that was not the case

for the raw data. Therefore, using a percentage table will usually
result in an incorrect answer.

Box 8.1 summarizes the critical information about lambda and
provides another example of its computation. Additional examples
can be found in the Exercises A and B at the end of the chapter.

Goodman and Kruskal's tau-b (τ_b) is similar to lambda. It uses a
method of prediction that will not fail to detect certain relationships, as sometimes occurs with lambda. *Phi* is another statistic for
measuring the strength of association between two nominal variables. It is discussed in detail later in this chapter.

Correlations for Ordinal Variables

Suppose we have a table with only two rows and two columns, and
both variables are ordinal. (Actually, since both variables would be
dichotomies, this could be any two-by-two table.) One way to evaluate the strength of the relationship would be to compute a statistic called *Yule's Q*. The formula for Yule's Q is:

$$Q = \frac{(a)(d) - (b)(c)}{(a)(d) + (b)(c)}$$

where a, b, c, and d are the frequencies in the four cells of the table
arranged as shown below.

		VARIABLE 1				INCOME	
		High	*Low*			*High*	*Low*
VARIABLE 2	*High*	a	b	POLITICAL	*High*	8	4
				INTEREST			
	Low	c	d		*Low*	2	6

Thus, to compute Yule's Q, one would simply multiply together the
two diagonal pairs of cases and then divide the difference between
these products by their sum. Using the frequencies in the table on
the right, the computation would be:

$$Q = \frac{(8)(6) - (4)(2)}{(8)(6) + (4)(2)} = \frac{48 - 8}{48 + 8} = \frac{40}{56} = +.71$$

BOX 8.1 Lambda and an Example of Its Computation

Statistic: Lambda (λ)

Type: Measure of association

Assumptions: Two nominal variables

Range: 0 to +1

Interpretation: Proportional reduction of error

Notes: Lambda is asymmetric. It should be computed only from raw frequencies, not from percentage tables.

Formula:

$$\text{Lambda} = \frac{b - a}{b}$$

where:

b = number of errors in predicting the dependent variable when the independent variable is not known.

a = number of errors in predicting the dependent variable when the independent variable is known.

Example: State Party Competition, by Region

		North East	Mid West	South	West	(Totals)
PARTY	High	2	8	1	5	(16)
COMPETITION	Medium	6	3	2	3	(14)
	Low	3	2	10	5	(20)

REGION

continues

---

continued

b = 16 + 14 = 30
a = 2 + 3 + 3 + 2 + 1 + 2 + 5 + 3 = 21

$$\text{Lambda} = \frac{b-a}{b} = \frac{30-21}{30} = \frac{9}{30} = .30$$

Conclusion: There is a definite relationship between region and party competition. States in the Midwest tend to have high party competion, while states in the South are the most likely to have low competition.

If all tables had only two rows and two columns, Yule's Q could be used every time. But since many tables are larger, we need to use a statistic such as *gamma*. Yule's Q is actually a special case of gamma and was presented first in order to show how gamma depends on the extent to which cases are clustered along one diagonal more than the other.

Gamma (γ) is a correlational statistic that measures the *strength of association between two ordinal variables*. It has a range of possible values from −1 to +1, with negative values indicating a negative relationship and zero indicating no relationship. Although it is not apparent from the computation procedure, the value for gamma may be interpreted as the proportionate reduction in error of prediction of one variable by the other, as was the case with lambda.

Unlike lambda, gamma is *symmetric*, that is, it does not make a distinction between the independent and dependent variables. *Gamma may also be computed from percentage tables.* The answer will be the same whether percentages or raw frequencies are used.

The formula for gamma is:

$$Q = \frac{P-Q}{P+Q}$$

where P is the number of pairs of cases consistent with a positive relationship and Q is the number of pairs inconsistent with a positive relationship.

The idea of "consistent pairs" and "inconsistent pairs" requires some explanation. Consider the following table.

	VARIABLE 1				INCOME		
	High	Med	Low		High	Med	Low
VARIABLE 2				**POLITICAL**			
High	a	b	c	**INTEREST** High	6	4	1
Medium	d	e	f	Medium	3	8	5
Low	g	h	i	Low	2	7	9

If there were a perfect positive relationship, every case that was higher on the first variable than another would also be higher on the second variable. Such comparisons are therefore "consistent" with a positive relationship. They would include a comparison of the high/high cases on each variable (cell a) with all of those in cells below and to the right (i.e., cells e, f, h, and i). Cells b, d, and e also have cases that are lower on both variables (i.e., below and to the right on the table). We are not really interested in individual comparisons, but only in how many such comparisons could be made; the number of such pairs can be calculated by multiplying the frequencies in each pair of "consistent" cells and adding up the total. In the example for income and political interest, the calculation would be P = 6(8 + 5 + 7 + 9) + 4(5 + 9) + 3(7 + 9) + 8(9) = 350.

The number of "inconsistent pairs" is the number of comparisons of cases that are higher on one variable but lower on the other. In the example above, cell c is lower on variable 1, but higher on variable 2 than cells d, e, h, and g. Cells b and f also may be compared to cases that are inconsistent, that is, below and to the left. Again, the total number of inconsistent pairs would be computed by multiplying the frequencies of all of such pairs and summing. In the income-political interest example, the calculation would be Q = 1(3 + 8 + 2 + 7) + 4(3 + 2) + 5 (2 + 7) + 8(2) = 101. Putting these numbers into the formula, we have:

$$\text{Gamma} = \frac{P - Q}{P + Q} = \frac{350 - 101}{350 + 101} = \frac{249}{451} = +.55$$

The value of .55 indicates that there is a moderately strong positive relationship between income and political interest; that is, people with higher incomes tend to have more political interest.

Thus the computation of gamma is the same as that of Yule's Q except that there are more possible comparisons. Note that whenever Q, the number of inconsistent pairs, is greater than P, the number of consistent pairs, the value of gamma will be negative.

Gamma, like lambda, has some drawbacks. One is that it ignores instances where there are "ties," that is, where cases are the same on one variable but different on the other. The effect can be seen in a table like this one:

		INCOME	
		High	*Low*
POLITICAL	*High*	5	5
INTEREST	*Low*	0	1

The value of gamma for this table would be a "perfect" +1, even though the relationship might better be described as a weak one. For this reason, a similar statistic, *Kendall's tau-b*, may be used. Kendall's tau-b is essentially the same as gamma, but it adjusts the value to take account of ties. The computed value of Kendall's tau-b will usually be less than but never greater than the value of gamma for the same table.

Box 8.2 summarizes the critical information about gamma and provides another example of its computation. Additional examples can be found in Exercises A and B at the end of the chapter.

Chi-Square: A Significance Test

The most commonly used test of significance for contingency tables is *chi-square (χ^2)*. Since it assumes that the variables are *nominal*, it is *always appropriate* as far as level of measurement is concerned. However, like all significance tests, the results are meaningful only if the data come from a *random sample*.

Unlike any of the other statistics we have presented, chi-square has a range of 0 to N, where N is the total number of cases in the table. This would make chi-square difficult to interpret, except that we rarely make use of the chi-square value directly. Rather, as we will see below, another step is taken to determine the associated

BOX 8.2 Information About Gamma and an Example of Its Computation

Statistic: Gamma (γ)

Type: Measure of association

Assumptions: Two ordinal variables

Range: −1 to +1

Interpretation: Proportional reduction of error

Formula:

$$Gamma = \frac{P - Q}{P + Q}$$

where:

P = number of pairs of cases consistent with a positive relationship.

Q = number of pairs of cases not consistent with a positive relationship.

Example: Voter turnout, by age

	AGE				
TURNOUT	*60 & Older*	*50–59*	*40–49*	*30–39*	*18–29*
Voter	12	13	14	9	7
Nonvoter	9	6	7	11	14

P=12(6+7+11+14) + 13(7+11+14) + 14(11+14) + 9(14) = 1,348
Q=7(9+6+7+11) + 9(9+6+7) + 14(9+6) + 13(9) = 810

continues

---

continued

$$\text{Gamma} = \frac{P-Q}{P+Q} = \frac{1,348-810}{1,348+810} = \frac{538}{2,158} = .25$$

Conclusion: This indicates that there is a moderately weak positive relationship between age and turnout. The older people are, the more likely they are to be voters.

---

probability—which is always the end product of a significance test. Chi-square *must be computed from raw frequencies*, not from a table expressed in percentages.

The formula for chi-square is:

$$\text{Chi}^2 = \sum \frac{(f_o - f_e)^2}{f_e}$$

where f_o refers to the *observed frequency* of each cell, that is, the numbers in the table, and f_e refers to the *expected frequency* of each cell, which is explained below. Sigma (Σ) is the summation sign, which indicates that one should perform the operation that follows for each of the cells and then add up the results.

To make this a little clearer, consider the example given in Box 8.3 showing the relationship between race and voting for a sample of 100 people. (The row, column, and table totals are shown because they will be needed in the computation.) *The observed frequencies (f_o) are the number of cases each cell would contain if there were no relationship between the variables*, given the existing totals for each row and each column. In this table it is easy to see how the expected frequencies are determined. Since the overall distribution of the vote is split evenly between the parties, a perfect nonrelationship would mean that both racial groups were evenly split as well.

In most tables, the value of the expected frequencies is not so obvious. Although one could take the proportion of total cases in each column and then multiply it by the column total, a quicker method that achieves the same result is this:

$$f_e = (row\ total \times column\ total) \div table\ total.$$

BOX 8.3 Computation of Chi-Square

	Observed Frequencies RACE					Expected Frequencies RACE		
	White	Non-white	*(totals)*		White	Non-white	*(totals)*
VOTE *Rep.*	40	10	(50)	**VOTE** *Rep.*	35	15	(50)
Dem.	30	20	(50)	*Dem.*	35	15	(50)
(totals)	(70)	(30)	(100)	*(totals)*	(70)	(30)	(100)

STEP 1 f_o	STEP 2 f_e	STEP 3 $f_o - f_e$	STEP 4 $(f_o - f_e)^2$	STEP 5 $(f_o - f_e)^2 / f_e$
40	50x70/100=35	40–35=5	$(5)^2=25$	25/35=0.71
10	50x30/100=15	10–15=–5	$(-5)^2=25$	25/15=1.67
30	50x70/100=35	30–35=–5	$(-5)^2=25$	25/35=0.71
20	50x30/100=15	20–15=5	$(5)^2=25$	25/15=1.67

STEP 6: Chi-square=4.76

For the upper left cell in the example (white/Republican), the computation would be f_e = (50 x 70) ÷ 100 = 35. The results for the other cells and the remaining steps in the table are shown in Box 8.3.

Setting up a table like that in Box 8.3 is recommended when computing chi-square. In step 1, the observed frequencies from the original table are listed. In step 2, the expected frequencies are computed as shown. In step 3, the difference between the first two columns is calculated. (Note that the $(f_o - f_e)$ column in step 3 must always total to zero.) In step 4, the values in the previous column are squared (which has the effect of eliminating the minus signs). In step 5, the squared values from the previous column are each divided by the value of f_e from step 2 in that line. Finally, step

6 entails totaling the values in step 5, which produces the value of chi-square. In this example, chi-square is 4.76.

As noted earlier, the value of chi-square does not mean much in itself. In order to determine the *probability*, it is necessary to consult a *probability of chi-square table*, a version of which is reproduced in Table 8.1. Before looking up the value of chi-square in the table, though, one more calculation is needed: The *degrees of freedom (df)* in the original table must be computed. This is done by multiplying the number of rows minus one by the number of columns minus one: df = (r − 1) (c − 1). In the above example, in which the table has two rows and two columns, the calculation is as follows: df = (2 − 1) (2 − 1) = 1.

This means that we look to row 1 in the degrees of freedom column on the left side of the table. From there, we look across the table to see where our chi-square value of 4.67 would best fit. We see that it falls between 3.841, which is in the .05 column, and 5.412, in the .02 column. This means that the probability (p) associated with our chi-square value is between that for 3.841, which is .05, and that for 5.412, which is .02; hence .05 > p > .02. Recalling the discussion of significance in Chapter 6, we can conclude that this relationship is significant because the probability of such a relationship occurring by chance in a random sample is less than .05.

When using a probability of chi-square table, you may sometimes find that the chi-square you have calculated is larger than any value in the appropriate line. This means that the probability is *less than* the lowest probability found in the table. In Table 8.1, this would mean that p < .001, which is highly significant. Similarly, if the calculated value is less than any value in the appropriate line of the table, the probability is *greater than* the highest probability shown and is therefore not significant.

Even when there is no relationship in a table, it may not be possible for observed frequencies to be exactly equal to expected frequencies, because the observed frequencies cannot be fractional values. When the number of cases is large, this problem will make no practical difference. But when the expected frequency for a cell is small, that is, less than five, some inflation of chi-square is possible. For that reason, an alternative method, such as *Fisher's exact test*, or a correction of chi-square for continuity, can be used. Many statistical computer programs provide this when needed.

TABLE 8.1   Probability of Chi-Square

Degrees of Freedom	.20	.10	.05	.02	.01	.001
1	1.642	2.706	3.841	5.412	6.635	10.827
2	3.219	4.605	5.991	7.834	9.210	13.815
3	4.642	6.251	7.815	9.837	11.341	16.268
4	5.989	7.779	9.488	11.668	13.277	18.465
5	7.289	9.236	11.070	13.388	15.086	20.517
6	8.558	10.645	12.595	15.033	16.812	22.457
7	9.803	12.017	14.067	16.622	18.475	24.322
8	11.030	13.362	15.507	18.168	20.090	26.125
9	12.242	14.684	16.919	19.679	21.666	27.877
10	13.422	15.987	18.307	21.161	23.209	29.588
11	14.631	17.275	19.675	22.618	24.725	31.264
12	15.812	18.549	21.026	24.054	26.217	32.909
13	16.985	19.812	22.362	25.472	27.688	34.528
14	18.151	21.064	23.685	26.873	29.141	36.123
15	19.311	22.037	24.996	28.259	30.578	37.697
16	20.465	23.542	26.296	29.633	32.000	39.252
17	21.615	24.769	27.587	30.995	33.409	40.790
18	22.760	25.989	28.869	32.346	34.805	42.312
19	23.900	27.204	30.144	33.687	36.191	43.820
20	25.038	28.412	31.410	35.020	37.566	45.315
21	26.171	29.615	32.671	36.343	38.932	46.797
22	27.301	30.813	33.924	37.659	40.289	48.268
23	28.429	32.007	35.172	38.968	41.638	49.728
24	29.553	33.196	36.415	40.270	42.980	51.179
25	30.675	34.382	37.652	41.566	44.314	52.620
26	31.795	35.563	38.885	42.856	45.642	54.052
27	32.912	36.741	40.113	44.140	46.963	55.476
28	34.027	37.916	41.337	45.419	48.278	56.893
29	35.139	39.087	42.557	46.693	49.588	58.302
30	36.250	40.256	43.773	47.962	50.892	59.703

continues

Box 8.4 summarizes information about chi-square and provides another example of its computation. Additional examples may be found in Exercises A and B at the end of the chapter.

Additional Correlations for Nominal Variables

As mentioned earlier, *phi* (*ϕ*) is another correlation for nominal data. Phi assumes that both variables are nominal, so it can be used with any contingency table. The range of possible values for phi is 0 to +1 for tables up to 2 x 2 (see the comment in connection with Cramer's V below). The interpretation for phi is that its squared value (phi^2) is equal to *the proportion of variance in one variable explained by the other*, a concept that is explained in Chapter 9. Indeed, for a 2 x 2 table, phi has the same value as the interval correlation Pearson's r (if one treated each dichotomous variable as interval and assigned numbers to the categories). Phi is *symmetric*; it makes no difference which variable is independent or dependent.

Phi can be computed in a number of ways, but the following simple formula may be used if chi-square has already been computed:

$$\text{Phi}^2 = \frac{\text{Chi}^2}{N}$$

where N is the total number of cases in the table. Recalling that the maximum possible value of chi-square is N, note that phi^2 is the ratio of the actual value of chi-square to the value it would have if there were a perfect relationship between the two variables.

Note that the formula calculates phi^2 (the squared value of phi). One can take the square root to obtain phi. However, phi^2 is often reported, since it is equal to the proportion of variance explained.

BOX 8.4 Information About Chi-Square and an Example of Its Computation

Statistic: Chi-square (χ^2)

Type: Significance test

Assumptions: Two nominal variables; random sampling

Range: 0 to N, where N is the total number of cases

Formula:

$$Chi^2 = \sum \frac{(f_o - f_e)^2}{f_e}$$

where:
f_o = observed (actual) frequency for each cell
f_e = expected frequency for each cell

Note: Chi-square must be computed from raw frequencies, not from a table expressed in terms of percentages.

Example: Form of city government and crime rate

Form of City Government

		Strong Mayor	Council Manager	Commission	(Totals)
CRIME					
RATE	*High*	7	3	9	(19)
	Medium	2	4	6	(12)
	Low	5	8	1	(14)
	(Totals)	(14)	(15)	(16)	(45)

continues

continued

f_o	f_e	f_o-f_e	$(f_o-f_e)^2$	$(f_o-f_e)^2/f_e$
7	19x14/45=5.91	7–5.91= 1.09	$(1.09)^2$= 1.19	1.19/5.91=0.20
3	19x15/45=6/33	3–3.63=–3.33	$(-3.33)^2$=11.09	11.09/6.33=0.57
9	19x16/45=6.76	9–6.76= 2.24	$(2.24)^2$= 5.02	5.02/6.76=0.74
2	12x14/45=3.73	2–3.73=–1.73	$(-1.73)^2$= 2.99	2.99/3/73=1.24
4	12x15/45=4.00	4–4.00= 0.00	$(0.00)^2$= 0.00	0.00/4.00=0.00
6	12x16/45=4.27	6–4.27= 1.73	$(1.73)^2$= 2.99	2.99/4.27=0.70
5	14x14/45=4.36	5–4.36= 0.64	$(0.64)^2$= 0.41	0.41/4.36=0.09
8	14x15/45=4.67	8–4.67= 3.33	$(3.33)^2$=11.09	11.09/4/98=2.37
1	14x16/45=4.98	1–4.98=–3.98	$(-3.98)^2$=15.80	15.80/3.17=3.17
				Chi-square =9.08

df = (3 – 1)(3 –) = 2   7.79 < Chi² < 9.488   .10 > p > .05

Conclusion: Since the probability of chi-square is greater than .05, it is not considered significant. We cannot conclude that there is any relationship between form of city government and the crime rate for the whole population from which this sample is drawn.

In the previous example for race and voting, the computation would be phi² = chi-square ÷ N = 4.76 ÷ 100 = 0.048. This shows that race explained a little less than 5 percent of the variance in voting. Although this is not an impressive figure in terms of strength of association, it must be emphasized that phi, like lambda, tends to have relatively low values, particularly compared to statistics like gamma. The value of lambda for the race/voting table is 0.24, and gamma would be 0.45.

One problem with phi is that for tables larger than two rows and two columns, it is possible for phi have a value larger than 1. Therefore, a number of statistics have been devised to adjust phi to avoid this difficulty. One of these is *Cramer's V*, calculated as follows:

$$V^2 = \frac{Phi^2}{Min(r-1, c-1)}$$

where Min(r − 1, c − 1) means the number of rows minus one or the number of columns minus one, whichever is less. In the race/voting example (a 2 x 2 table), r − 1 and c − 1 are both equal to 1, so V = phi, and this computation is unnecessary.

Box 8.5 summarizes the information about Phi and applies it to the example from Box 8.4.

Interpreting Contingency Tables Using Statistics

As stated earlier, statistics are a tool for helping us interpret our data. Bivariate statistics, such as those presented in this chapter, tell us something about relationships. But what different statistics tell us can be confusing.

Measures of association or correlations (such as lambda, gamma, and phi) tell us something about the strength of a relationship. But what is considered to be a "strong" association and what is a "weak" association? There is no simple answer to that question. Although some authors have suggested ranges, such as defining a gamma value of .70 or greater as "very strong," these ranges are arbitrary. Furthermore, there would have to be different lists for every statistic. Although the statistics have varying mathematical interpretations, the best approach for the novice is to think of them as *relative measures of strength*. This can be useful if one is comparing several relationships between similar pairs of variables, such as the correlation between the attitude of individuals on the abortion issue and their votes in several presidential elections, thus facilitating a decision as to which relationship was the strongest. But it is important to remember to *make direct comparisons only of the same statistical measure.* Comparing a gamma value with a lambda value, for example, is highly likely to be misleading.

When using ordinal statistics, such as gamma, it is very important to be aware that the order in which the categories appear in the rows and columns will determine whether the value is positive or negative, which shows the direction of the relationship. All of the examples in this chapter have the highest values of ordinal variables in the top row and the left column, thus ensuring that a positive relationship will produce a positive value for gamma. But tables are not always set up that way, particularly when produced by

---

**BOX 8.5   Information About Phi and
an Example of Its Computation**

Statistic: Phi (ϕ)

Type: Measure of association

Assumptions: Two nominal variables

Range: 0 to 1 (for a 2 × 2 table)

Formula:

$$Phi^2 = \frac{Chi^2}{N}$$

where N = the total number of cases in the table

Example: For the data in Box 8.4:

$$Phi^2 = \frac{Chi^2}{N} = \frac{9.08}{45} = .20$$

Conclusion: Phi^2 shows that 20 percent of the variance in crime rate is explained by the form of city government. This is a moderately strong relationship.

NOTE: Since the table was larger than 2 by 2, Cramer's V would be a more appropriate measure. $V^2 = 0.20 \div 2 = .10$

---

computers. Most statistical programs will put the first or lowest value in the left column and top row, and that will often be the code for the lowest actual value (e.g., age might be coded as 18–29 years = 1, 30–49 years = 2, etc.). To prevent this problem, always *look carefully at the contingency table.* One can then see what the direction of the relationship appears to be and what a positive or negative value of a correlation would mean.

Exercises

Exercise A

Using the data on education and ideology in the following table, complete items 1–10.

| | | EDUCATION | | | |
		College	H.S. Grad	Some H.S.	Grade School
IDEOLOGY	*Liberal*	50	60	20	10
	Conservative	20	60	30	20

1. Present the table in terms of percentages, using proper form.
2. Is it appropriate to compute lambda for these data? Why or why not?
3. If appropriate, compute lambda.
4. Is it appropriate to compute gamma for these data? Why or why not?
5. If appropriate, compute gamma.
6. What assumptions would have to be made to use chi-square as a test of significance for these data?
7. Compute chi-square and determine its probability. Is this significant?
8. Is it appropriate to compute phi for these data? Would Cramer's V be a better measure?
9. If appropriate, compute phi.
10. On the basis of all of these computations, draw a conclusion about the relationship.

Exercise B

Using the data on income and vote in the following table, complete items 1–10 from Exercise A.

| | | INCOME | | |
		Over $50,00	$25,000– 50,000	Under $25,000
VOTE	*Dole*	22	19	8
	Clinton	11	23	15
	Perot	9	7	3
	Nonvoter	17	25	23

Exercise C

For each of the following pairs of variables, identify all of the following statistics that would be appropriate: lambda, gamma, and phi.

1. Opinion on welfare spending (increase, keep the same, decrease) and defense spending (increase, keep the same, decrease)
2. Largest minority group (African American, Hispanic, Asian, Native American) and crime rate (high, medium, low)
3. Social class (upper, middle, working) and vote (Republican, Democrat)
4. Dominant religion (Christianity, Islam, Buddhism, Hinduism, other) and per capita GNP (up to $999, $1,000 to $2,999, $,3000 and up)
5. Gender (male, female) and vote (Bush, Clinton, Perot)

Suggested Answers to Exercises

Exercise A

1.

			EDUCATION		
			H.S.	Some	Grade
		College	Grad	H.S.	School
IDEOLOGY	*Liberal*	71%	50%	40%	33%
	Conservative	29	50	60	67
		100%	100%	100%	100%
		N=70	N=120	N=50	N=30

2. Yes. Lambda requires only nominal variables, so it may always be used.

3. b = 130
   a = 20 + 60 + 20 + 10 = 110

$$\text{Lambda} = \frac{350 - 110}{130} = \frac{20}{130} = .15$$

4. Yes. Gamma requires two ordinal variables. Education is ordinal and ideology is a dichotomy, so it may be treated as ordinal.

5. P = 50(60 + 30 + 20) = 60(30 + 20) + 20(20) = 8,900
   Q = 10(20 + 60 + 30) + 20(20 + 60) + 60(20) = 3,900

$$\text{Gamma} = \frac{8,900 - 3,900}{890 - 3,900} = \frac{5,000}{12,800} = +.39$$

6. In terms of level of measurement, chi-square requires only nominal variables, so it is always appropriate. But it is valid as a significance test only if the data come from a random sample.

7.

f_o	f_e	$f_o - f_e$	$(f_o - f_e)^2$	$(f_o - f_e)^2/f_e$
50	36.3	13.7	187.7	5.17
60	62.2	−2.2	4.8	0.08
20	25.9	−5.9	34.8	1.34
10	15.6	−5.6	31.4	2.01
20	33.7	−13.7	187.7	5.57
60	57.8	2.2	4.8	0.08
30	24.1	5.9	34.8	1.44
20	14.4	5.6	31.4	2.18
				17.87 = chi-square

df = (2 − 1)(4 − 1) = 3, 16.268 < chi², .001 > p (significant)

8. Since phi requires only nominal variables, it is always appropriate. Since Min(r − 1, c − 1) = 1, Cramer's V would be the same as phi.

9. Phi² = 17.87 ÷ 270 = .07

10. There is a moderately weak significant positive relationship between education and liberal ideology. The more education people have, they more likely they are to be liberal.

Exercise B

1. Income

		INCOME		
		Over	*$25,000–*	*Under*
		$50,000	*50,000*	*$25,000*
VOTE	*Dole*	37%	26%	16%
	Clinton	19	31	31
	Perot	15	9	6
	Nonvoter	29	34	47
		100%	100%	100%
		N=59	N=74	N=49

2. Yes. Lambda requires only nominal variables, so it may always be used.

3. b = 49 + 49 + 19 = 117
    a = 11 + 9 + 17 + 19 + 23 + 7 + 8 + 15 + 3 = 112

$$\text{Lambda} = \frac{117 - 112}{117} = \frac{5}{117} = .04$$

4. No. Gamma requires two ordinal variables. Although income is ordinal, vote is nominal and not a dichotomy.

5. Not applicable.

6. In terms of level of measurement, chi-square requires only nominal variables, so it always appropriate. But it is valid as a significance test only if the data come from a random sample.

7.

f_o	f_e	$f_o - f_e$	$(f_o - f_e)^2$	$(f_o - f_e)^2/f_e$
22	15.9	6.1	37.21	2.34
19	19.9	−0.9	0.81	0.04
8	13.2	−5.2	27.04	2.05
11	15.9	−4.9	24.01	1.51
23	19.9	3.1	9.61	0.48
15	13.2	1.8	3.24	0.25
9	6.2	2.8	7.84	1.26
7	7.7	−0.7	0.49	0.06
3	5.1	−2.1	4.41	0.86
17	21.1	−4.1	16.81	0.80
25	26.4	−1.4	1.96	0.07
23	17.5	5.5	30.25	1.73
				10.19 = chi-square

$df = (3 - 1)(4 - 1) = 6$, $8.588 <$ chi-square < 10.645, $.20 < p < .10$ (not significant)

8. Since phi requires only nominal variables, it is always appropriate. Since $Min(r - 1, c - 1) = 2$, Cramer's V would be a better measure.

9. $Phi^2 = 10.19 \div 182 = .06$
$V = .06 \div 2 = .03$

10. There is a weak relationship that is not significant. For the sample data, there is a tendency for people with higher incomes to be more likely to vote for Dole and Perot, and the lower people's income, the more likely they are to vote for Clinton or to be nonvoters.

Exercise C

1. Both variables are ordinal, so lambda, phi, and gamma could all be used.
2. Crime rate is ordinal, and largest minority group is nominal and not a dichotomy, so only lambda and phi could be used (and Cramer's V would be better than phi).
3. Social class is ordinal and vote is a dichotomy, so lambda, gamma, and phi could all be used.
4. Per capita GNP is ordinal, and religion is nominal and not a dichotomy, so only lambda and phi could be used (and Cramer's V would be a better measure than phi).
5. Gender is a dichotomy, and vote is nominal and is not a dichotomy, so only lambda and phi could be used.

9

Interval Statistics

In this chapter we will look at statistics that evaluate the relationship between two interval variables. These statistics are derived from a procedure called *regression*; they and their multivariate extensions (covered in Chapter 10) are by far the most commonly used statistics in contemporary political science research.

The Regression Line

The idea of regression is best illustrated with the use of scattergrams, which were introduced in Chapter 6. The examples of "perfect" relationships shown there were instances in which all of the points representing the cases fell along single straight lines. If all relationships between variables were perfect in that way—that is, perfectly correlated—we would not need many statistics. But in the imperfect world of the social sciences, most relationships are far from perfect, and even careful visual inspection of a scattergram will tell us only so much about the relationship between the variables plotted.

The key idea of regression is that there is a single, "best-fitting," line that describes the relationship between the variables better than any other line would. Let us assume, for now, that this line is a straight one. Regression statistics define this as the *least-squares line*, that is, *if we the measure the distance of each case from that line and square each value, then the total will be less than what the total would be for any other line*. Fortunately, we do not have to do this with a ruler; there are formulas to determine the exact location of the line and a measure of how good a fit the line is to the points.

Any straight line can be completely described by two facts: the location of a single point through which it passes and the slope or angle at which it rises or falls. The equation for a straight line may be written as Y = a + bX, where Y is the dependent variable, X is the independent variable, a is the height of the line where it crosses the y-axis, and b is the slope. Box 9.1 shows an example of a scattergram with the least-squares line. The equation for the line is Y = 0.7 + 1.1X. This means that the line crosses the y-axis at a height of 0.7 and goes up by 1.1 for every increase of 1 unit in X.

How did we determine the values of a and b? There are formulas for each. The value of b, the slope, is calculated as follows:

$$b = \frac{N\Sigma XY - (\Sigma X)(\Sigma Y)}{N\Sigma X^2 - (\Sigma X)^2}$$

where X and Y are values of the independent and dependent variables and N is the number of cases. Sigma (Σ), the summation sign, indicates that one must add up the value for all cases. Note that ΣXY is *not* the same as $(\Sigma X)(\Sigma Y)$. ΣXY means that one must first multiply the value of X by the value of Y for each case and then add up these products for all cases. $(\Sigma X)(\Sigma Y)$ means that one first adds up the original values of X and Y and then multiplies the products. Similarly, ΣX^2 is different from $(\Sigma X)^2$.

To calculate b, a, and Pearson's r (discussed below), we need to find the value of five sums: those of the original values of X (i.e., ΣX) and Y (i.e., ΣY), those of the squared values of each variable (i.e., ΣX^2 and ΣY^2), and that of the product of X times Y (i.e., ΣXY). We also use N, the number of cases. It is useful to set up a table like the one below, which uses the data for the scattergram in Box 9.1 to illustrate the procedure.

	STEP 1		STEP 2	STEP 3	STEP 4
	X	Y	X^2	Y^2	XY
	1	2	1	4	2
	2	3	4	9	6
	3	3	9	9	9
	4	6	16	36	24
	5	6	25	36	30
Sums:	15	20	55	94	71

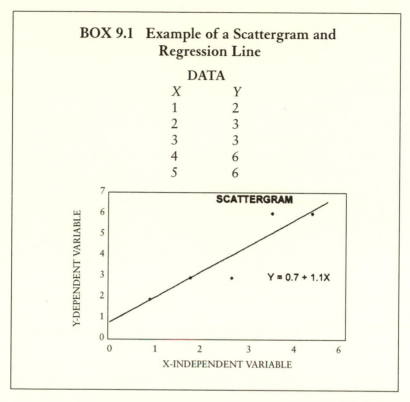

BOX 9.1   Example of a Scattergram and Regression Line

DATA

X	Y
1	2
2	3
3	3
4	6
5	6

SCATTERGRAM

$Y = 0.7 + 1.1X$

Y-DEPENDENT VARIABLE

X-INDEPENDENT VARIABLE

In step 1, we take the original values of X and Y and add up each column, giving us $\Sigma X = 15$ and $\Sigma Y = 20$. In step 2, we square each of the values of X and add up the column to get $\Sigma X^2 = 55$. In step 3, we do the same for the original values of Y to get $\Sigma Y = 94$. In step 4, we multiply the value of X by the value of Y for each case and then add up the column to get $\Sigma XY = 71$. Now we place these sums, along with the number of cases (N = 5) in the formula for b.

$$b = \frac{N\Sigma XY - (\Sigma X)(\Sigma Y)}{N(\Sigma X^2) - (\Sigma X)^2} = \frac{5(71) - (15)(20)}{5(55) - (15)^2} = \frac{355 - 200}{275 - 225} = \frac{55}{50} = 1.1$$

To calculate the value of a, often called the *constant* or the *y-intercept*, the formula is:

$$a = \frac{\Sigma Y - b\Sigma X}{N}$$

Thus, using the figures for this example, we have:

$$a = \frac{\Sigma Y - b\Sigma X}{N} = \frac{20 - 1.1(15)}{5} = \frac{20 - 16.5}{5} = \frac{35}{5} = 0.7$$

Another example of these computations is shown in Box 9.2. The slope of the line, b, gives us a very important piece of information. *The slope is a direct measure of the effect of the independent variable on the dependent variable.* And whether it has a plus or a minus sign tells us whether the relationship is positive or negative. However, it has the disadvantage of being highly dependent on the units in which the variables are measured. Age can be measured is days and months as well as years; income in dollars, thousands of dollars, other currencies, and so on. Making a different choice of units could drastically affect the value of b. For that reason, it is common to compute a standardized version of the slope called *beta*, a measure that will be discussed in Chapter 10.

Pearson's r

Although the slope of the line is important, it does not give us a measure of strength of association in the way that other measures such as gamma and phi do. For that we use a statistic called the *Pearson product-moment correlation*, or *Pearson's r*. (It is so widely used that it is often reported simply as "r," and references only to a "correlation" probably refer to it as well.)

Pearson's r assumes that there are *two interval variables*. Its range is from −1 to +1. It is a measure of association, that is, of the strength of the relationship. Essentially, it measures how closely the case points cluster around the regression line. In this sense, it is a measure of how good a predictor one variable is of the other. As was the case with Phi^2, r^2 *is equal to the proportion of variance in one variable explained by the other.*

This idea of "explained variance" is a crucial one in statistical theory. If we knew nothing about any other variables, then the best predictor of the value of every case of Y, the dependent variable, would be the mean value of Y. For example, in Box 9.1, picture a horizontal line across the scattergram at the height of the mean, which in this example is 4 (computed by adding up the values of Y and dividing by N). The total variance in Y would be the sum of the squared deviations of the actual cases from this mean line. To the

BOX 9.2 Example of Regression and Computations of b and a

% URBAN X	% TURNOUT Y	X2	Y2	XY
0	80	0	6,400	0
100	30	10,000	900	3,000
90	50	8,100	2,500	4,500
20	70	400	4,900	1,400
50	60	2,500	3,600	3,000
30	40	900	1,600	1,200
40	50	1,600	2,500	2,000
70	50	4,900	2,500	3,500
60	30	3,600	900	1,800
40	40	1,600	1,600	1,600
SUMS: 500	500	33,600	27,400	22,000

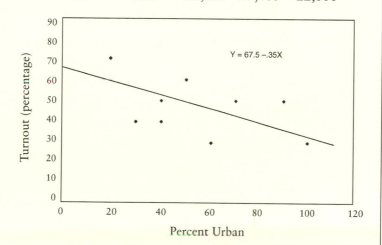

$$b = \frac{N \sum XY - (\sum X)(\sum Y)}{N \sum X^2 - (\sum X)^2} = \frac{10(22,000) - (500)(500)}{10(33,600) - (500)^2}$$

$$= \frac{220,000 - 250,000}{336,000 - 250,000} = \frac{-30,000}{86,000} = -.35$$

$$a = \frac{\sum Y - b \sum X}{N} = \frac{500 - (-.35)(500)}{10} = \frac{500 + 175}{10} = \frac{675}{10} = 67.5$$

extent that an independent variable, X, is of some value as a predictor, then the deviations around the least-squares regression line will be less. Pearson's r^2 directly measures this improvement in prediction.

The formula for Pearson's r is similar to that for b and a in that it uses the sums of the values, their squares, and their products:

$$r = \frac{N\Sigma XY - (\Sigma X)(\Sigma Y)}{\sqrt{\left[N\Sigma X^2 - (\Sigma X)^2\right]\left[N\Sigma Y^2 - (\Sigma Y)^2\right]}}$$

Although it may not seem immediately obvious from a look at the formula, note that Pearson's r is *symmetrical*. Although the formula requires that one variable be designated as independent (X) and the other as dependent (Y), the answer will be the same no matter which role the variables are placed in.

To calculate r for the previous example, take the results of steps 1 through 4, which yielded $X = 15$, $Y = 20$, $X^2 = 60$, $Y^2 = 94$, $XY = 71$, and $N = 5$. Substituting these values into the formula, we have:

$$r = \frac{5(71) - (15)(20)}{\sqrt{\left[5(55) - (15)^2\right]\left[5(94) - (20)^2\right]}} = \frac{355 - 300}{\sqrt{(275 - 225)(470 - 400)}}$$

$$= \frac{55}{\sqrt{(50)(70)}} = \frac{55}{\sqrt{3500}} = \frac{55}{59.2} = +.93$$

This value or r, .93, shows that there is, as we would expect from the scattergram, a very strong positive relationship. The proportion of variance explained is indicated by r^2, which is .86.

We can also test the significance of Pearson's r for significance using the *F-ratio*, or *F-test*. This test assumes, of course, that the data come from a random sample.

The value of F is computed as follows:

$$F = \frac{r^2(N-2)}{1-r^2}$$

Using the values of r = .93 and N = 5 from the previous example,

$$F = \frac{(.93)^2(5-2)}{1-(.93)^2} = \frac{.86(3)}{1-.86} = \frac{2.58}{.14} = 18.43$$

This value of F, like chi-square values, requires a table to determine the probability, which is reproduced in Table 9.1. The table is used much like the chi-square table, though in this one, N − 2 is the number of degrees of freedom. For this example, we go down to line 3 and look across. Our F value of 18.43 would fall between 10.13 and 34.12. Therefore, the probability would be between .05 and .01 and would be considered significant. This illustrates the fact that even a tiny random sample of five cases can produce a significant correlation—if that correlation happens to be very strong, as this one was.

Note in Table 9.1 that in the N − 2 column, after the values reach 30, they skip to 40, 60, 120, and then to infinity. This is simply for convenience; as inspection of the values in the body of the table shows, the numbers change very little, so including intermediate values would be a waste of space. When you have an N − 2 value that does not appear in the table, the best way to proceed would be to use the next lowest available value. Thus if N − 2 were 50, one could use the figures for line 40, and this would almost always lead to the correct conclusion.

Box 9.3 summarizes the critical information about Pearson's r and presents an additional example of its computation and the F-test. Other examples can be found in the exercises at the end of the chapter.

Nonlinear Relationships

Thus far we have assumed that a "perfect" relationship between two interval variables would take the form of a straight line on a scattergram. But this is not necessarily the case for perfect relationships in the real world. Consider Figure 9.1, which shows the path of an object hurled in the air. It is a perfect relationship in that knowing the horizontal distance traveled enables you to predict the height perfectly. However, this path is not described by a straight line, but by a curve (a parabola). This illustrates why it is important always to look at a scattergram when investigating interval re-

TABLE 9.1   Probability of F

	PROBABILITY LEVELS		
N – 2	.05	.01	.001
1	161.4	4,052.00	405,284.00
2	18.51	98.49	998.50
3	10.13	34.12	167.50
4	7.71	21.20	74.14
5	6.61	16.26	47.04
6	5.99	13.74	35.51
7	5.59	12.25	29.22
8	5.32	11.26	25.42
9	5.12	10.56	22.86
10	4.96	10.04	21.04
11	4.84	9.65	19.69
12	4.75	9.33	18.64
13	4.67	9.07	17.81
14	4.60	8.86	17.14
15	4.54	8.68	16.59
16	4.49	8.53	16.12
17	4.45	8.40	15.72
18	4.41	8.28	15.38
19	4.38	8.18	15.08
20	4.35	8.10	14.82
21	4.32	8.02	14.59
22	4.30	7.94	14.38
23	4.28	7.88	14.19
24	4.26	7.82	14.03
25	4.24	7.77	13.88

continues

continued

26	4.22	7.72	13.74
27	4.21	7.68	13.61
28	4.20	7.64	13/50
29	4.18	7.60	13.39
30	4.17	7.56	13.29
40	4.08	7.31	12.61
60	4.00	7.08	11.97
120	3.92	6.85	11.38
INFINITY	3.84	6.64	10.83

NOTE: This table is designed for testing significance where there is only one independent variable. Table 10.1 may be used for multiple and partial correlations. Larger tables can be found in many comprehensive statistics texts.

SOURCE: Ronald A. Fisher and Frank Yates, *Statistical Tables for Biological, Agricultural, and Medical Research, Sixth Edition* (Edinburgh: Oliver and Boyd, 1963), pp.53, 55, 57. © R. A. Fisher and F. Yates. Reprinted by permission of Pearson Education, Limited.

lationships. In an example like this one, the linear correlation and regression statistics described in the previous section (b and r) would indicate that there was no relationship between height and distance. Viewing the scattergram could prevent accepting that erroneous conclusion. A variety of techniques—all beyond the scope of this book—can be used to analyze nonlinear or *curvilinear* relationships. (The simplest approach for this example would be to divide the data at the midpoint of the independent variable and analyze each half separately with linear regression, which would then yield a reasonably correct analysis.) But if one never looked at the scattergram, the need for this might never be apparent.

BOX 9.3 Information About Pearson's r, the F-Test, and an Example of Their Computation

Statistic: Pearson's r

Type: Measure of association

Assumptions: Two interval variables

Range: −1 to +1

Interpretation: Proportion of variance explained (r^2)

Formula:

$$r = \frac{N\sum XY - (\sum X)(\sum Y)}{\sqrt{\left[N\sum X^2 - (\sum X)^2\right]\left[N\sum Y^2 - (\sum Y)^2\right]}}$$

Example (Continued from Box 9.2)

$\sum X=500$ $\sum Y=500$ $\sum X^2=33,600$ $\sum Y^2=27,400$ $\sum XY=22,000$
$N=10$

F-test:

$$r = \frac{10(22,000) - (500)(500)}{\sqrt{\left[10(33,600) - (500)^2\right]\left[10(27,400) - (500)^2\right]}}$$

$$r = \frac{220,000 - 250,000}{\sqrt{(336,000 - 250,000)(274,000 - 250,000)}}$$

$$r = \frac{-30,000}{\sqrt{(86,000)(24,000)}} = \frac{-30,000}{\sqrt{2,064,000}} = \frac{-30,000}{45,431} = -.66$$

F-test
Assumptions: Random sampling

Formula: $F = \dfrac{r^2 (N-2)}{1 - r^2}$

continues

continued

Example (from above)

$$F = \frac{(-.66)^2 (10-2)}{1-(.66)^2} = \frac{.44(8)}{1-.44} = \frac{3.53}{.56} = 6.28$$

From Table 9.1:

5.32 < F < 11.26, so .05 > p > .01 (significant)

Conclusion: There is a strong significant negative relationship between % Urban and % Turnout. The more urban an area, the lower its level of turnout.

Relationships Between Interval and Nominal Variables

There are many instances where one may want to evaluate the relationship between a nominal or ordinal variable and an interval variable. Typically this occurs when we are comparing two groups defined by the nominal or ordinal variable to see whether they are different on the interval variable. We might, for example, have a sample of individuals and wish to determine whether the difference in income between males and females was large enough to be considered significant. A number of statistical tests could be used to do this, such as the *t-test* and *difference of means*. Although significance tests are the main statistics used for the comparisons of groups, a measure of strength of association similar to Pearson's r called *eta* is useful where there is a possibility that the relationship is curvilinear.

Exercises

Answers to these exercises follow. It is suggested that you attempt to complete the exercises before looking at the answers.

FIGURE 9.1   Example of a curvilinear relationship

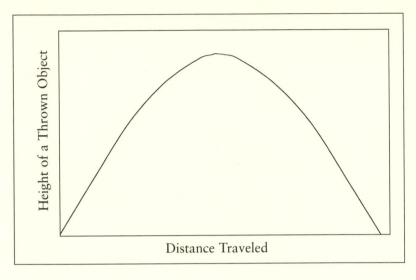

Exercise A

Using the data in the following table on the relationship between years of education and number of times a person voted in the past five elections, complete items 1–5.

Years of Education	# of Votes	Years of Education	# of Votes	Years of Education	# of Votes
8	4	12	3	16	4
9	1	13	3	10	2
10	0	12	2	11	3
16	5	12	4	12	5
15	5	14	4	12	0

1. Draw a scattergram. What sort of relationship does there appear to be?
2. Compute b and a and draw the regression line on the scattergram.
3. Compute Pearson's r.
4. Conduct the F-test and determine the significance.
5. Draw a conclusion about the relationship.

Exercise B

Using the data in the following table on the relationship between per capita income (in thousands of dollars) and percentage of a nation's budget spent on defense, complete items 1–5 from Exercise A.

Income	Defense	Income	Defense	Income	Defense
10	10	30	15	12	11
3	5	25	16	9	3
2	1	7	8	22	14
1	3	6	7	15	15
20	15	4	6		

Exercise C

Suppose a random sample of seventy-two counties showed a value for Pearson's r of .13 between urbanization and crime. Conduct an F-test to determine the significance of this relationship.

Suggested Answers to Exercises

Exercise A

1.

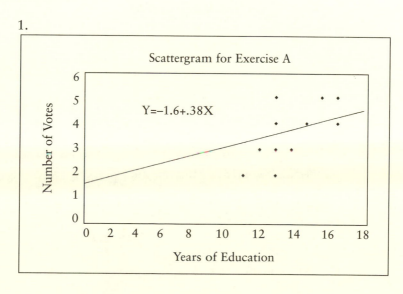

Scattergram for Exercise A

$Y=-1.6+.38X$

2.

EDUCATION AND VOTES					
X	Y	X^2	Y^2	XY	
8	4	64	16	32	
9	1	81	1	9	
10	0	100	0	0	
16	5	256	25	80	
15	5	225	25	75	
12	3	144	9	36	
13	3	169	9	39	
12	2	144	4	24	
12	4	144	16	48	
14	4	196	16	56	
16	4	256	16	64	
10	2	100	4	20	
11	3	121	9	33	
12	5	144	25	6	
12	0	144	0	0	
182	45	2,288	175	576	(TOTALS)

$$b = \frac{15(576) - (182)(45)}{15(2,288) - (182)^2} = \frac{8,640 - 8,190}{34,320 - 33,124} = 1\frac{450}{1,196} = +.38$$

$$a = \frac{45 - .38(182)}{15} = \frac{45 - 69.2}{15} = \frac{-24.2}{15} = -1.6$$

3.

$$r = \frac{15(576) - (182)(45)}{\sqrt{\left[15(2,288) - (182)^2\right]\left[15(175) - (45)^2\right]}}$$

$$= \frac{8,640 - 8,190}{\sqrt{(34,320 - 33,124)(2,625 - 2,025)}}$$

$$r = \frac{450}{\sqrt{(1,196)(600)}} = \frac{450}{847.1} = +.53$$

4.

$$F = \frac{(.53)^2(15-2)}{1-(.53)^2} = \frac{(.28)(13)}{1-.28} = \frac{3.65}{.72} = 5.07$$

$4.67 < F < 9.07$, so $.05 > p > .01$ (significant!)

5. There is a strong and significant positive relationship between education and frequency of voting. The more education people have, the more elections they tend to vote
in. If the data were from a random sample, we could conclude that this positive relationship occurs in the population from which the sample was drawn.

Exercise B

1.

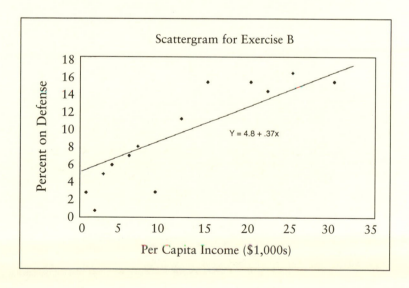

Scattergram for Exercise B
$Y = 4.8 + .37x$
Percent on Defense
Per Capita Income ($1,000s)

INCOME AND DEFENSE

X	Y	X^2	Y^2	XY
10	10	100	100	100
3	5	9	25	15
2	1	4	1	2
1	3	1	9	3
20	15	400	225	300
30	15	900	225	300
25	16	625	256	400
7	8	49	64	56
6	7	36	49	42
4	6	16	36	24
12	11	144	121	132
9	3	81	9	27
22	14	484	196	308
15	15	225	225	225
166	129	3,074	1,541	1,934

$N = 14$

$$b = \frac{14(1,934) - (166)(129)}{14(3,074) - (166)^2} = \frac{27,076 - 21,414}{43,036 - 27,556} = \frac{5,662}{15,480} = +.37$$

3.

$$a = \frac{129 - (.37)(166)}{14} = \frac{67.6}{14} = +4.48$$

$$r = \frac{14(1,934) - (166)(129)}{\sqrt{\left[14(3,074) - (166)^2\left[14(1,341) - (129)^2\right]\right]}}$$

$$= \frac{27,076 - 21,414}{\sqrt{(43,036 - 27,556)(21,574 - 16,641)}}$$

$$r = \frac{5,662}{\sqrt{76,362,840}} = \frac{5,662}{8,738.6} = +.64$$

4.

$$F = \frac{(.64)^2 (14-2)}{1-(.64)^2} = \frac{.42(12)}{1-.42} = \frac{5.04}{.58} = 8.68$$

$4.75 < F < 9.33$, so $.05 < p < .01$ (significant)

5. There is a strong and significant positive relationship between a nation's per capita income and defense spending. The higher the income, the more spent on defense. If these data were from a random sample of nations, we could conclude that there is a positive relationship between per capita income and defense spending among nations in general.

Exercise C

$$F = \frac{(.13)^2 (72-2)}{1-(.13)^2} = \frac{.017(70)}{1-.017} = \frac{1.18}{.983} = 1.2$$

$F < 4.00$, so $p > .05$ (NOT significant)

Although there is a relationship between urbanization and crime for the counties in this sample, we cannot conclude that there is any relationship for the whole population from which this sample was drawn.

10

Multivariate Statistics

This chapter presents techniques for dealing with the analysis of the relationship between *three or more variables*. Given the nature of the social and political world, we frequently face situations where there are several, or even many, possible causes of some phenomenon. Just think how many different factors might go into an individual's voting decision, ranging from the party identification adopted in childhood, to a variety of attitudes and opinions, to news broadcasts and campaign appeals immediately before the election. Sorting out potential independent variables is largely a matter of controlling—and, as you know from Chapter 3, the use of control variables is essential in the correlational research design. In this chapter you will learn techniques for imposing those controls. We will begin with the method for nominal and ordinal category variables and then turn to interval techniques.

Controlling with Contingency Tables

As you have already learned, relationships between categorized nominal and ordinal variables are analyzed using contingency tables. Contingency tables also may be used to control for third variables. This is fairly easily done: For each category of the control variable, a table is constructed showing the relationship between the independent and dependent variables. Each of these tables may then be presented in terms of percentages and appropriate statistics may be calculated. Note that to evaluate the effect of the control variable, it is necessary to compare the control tables to a table without a control variable.

Box 10.1 illustrates this procedure for a simple case in which all variables are dichotomized. Suppose we wanted to see whether the relationship between religion and voting was affected by an individual's income level. First we would construct a table showing the relationship between the independent variable (religion) and the dependent variable (vote). Then we would construct the same table for each category (high and low) of the control variable (income). Note that the frequencies for each combination of the independent and dependent variables (such as Protestant Republican) in the control tables add up to the frequency in the original table. Each table could then be expressed in terms of percentages and appropriate statistics computed. For this example, lambda, gamma, and phi are reported. (Assuming the data were from a random sample, chi-square could have been used, but with the small number of cases it would not have been significant.)

What does the example in Box 10.1 show? For all of the cases, there is a weak relationship between religion and vote. Protestants tend to vote Republican, and Catholics tend to vote Democratic. When we look at each of the control tables, the same is true for both higher- and lower-income respondents. The statistics measuring the strength of the association vary slightly, but basically they show the same relationship as in the original table. This outcome demonstrates that the control variable (income) had little or no effect on the relationship between the independent variable (religion) and the dependent variable (vote). In other words, the effect of religious preference on the vote was *not* due to a person's income.

What Can Happen When You Control

Several things can happen to a relationship between two variables when you control for a third variable. Box 10.2 illustrates this with an example of the relationship between income and voting as we control for four other characteristics of the individuals. The "original" table for all of the cases (part A) shows that there is a moderately strong, but significant, relationship: People with higher incomes were more likely to vote Republican.

The first possible outcome of controlling is that nothing happens, that is, the relationship is unchanged. This is shown in part B of Box 10.2 when we control for gender. The tables for males and females are exactly the same and therefore have the same strength of relationship. (The chi-square values are smaller because the control ta-

---

BOX 10.1 Controlling Using Contingency Tables

A. Data

INCOME	RELIG'N	VOTE	INCOME	RELIG'N	VOTE	INCOME	RELIG'N	VOTE
High	Prot.	Rep.	High	Cath.	Rep.	High	Prot.	Rep.
High	Cath.	Dem.	Low	Prot.	Rep.	Low	Cath.	Dem.
Low	Prot.	Rep.	High	Cath.	Dem.	Low	Prot.	Rep.
Low	Cath.	Dem.	Low	Prot.	Dem.	High	Cath.	Dem.
High	Prot.	Dem.	Low	Cath.	Rep.	Low	Prot.	Dem.

B. Frequencies

CONTROLLING FOR INCOME

ALL CASES (NO CONTROLS) RELIGION			HIGH INCOME RELIGION			LOW INCOME RELIGION		
VOTE	Prot	Cath	VOTE	Prot	Cath	VOTE	Prot	Cath
Rep	5	2	Rep	2	1	Rep	3	1
Dem	3	5	Dem	1	3	Dem	2	2

C. Percentage Tables and Statistics

CONTROLLING FOR INCOME

ALL CASES (NO CONTROLS) RELIGION			HIGH INCOME RELIGION			LOW INCOME RELIGION		
VOTE	Prot	Cath	VOTE	Prot	Cath	VOTE	Prot	Cath
Rep	62%	29%	Rep	67%	25%	Rep	60%	33%
Dem	38	71	Dem	33	75	Dem	40	67
	100%	100%		100%	100%		100%	100%
N=	8	7		3	4		5	3

Lambda = .29	Lambda = .33	Lambda = .25
Gamma = +.61	Gamma = +.71	Gamma = +.50
Phi^2 = .12	Phi^2 = .17	Phi^2 = .19

---

bles are based on fewer cases.) In real-life examples the percentages would rarely stay exactly the same, but the important thing is that the measures of strength are not much altered. This is the same outcome as in the example in Box 10.1. When this happens, we can conclude that the apparent relationship between the independent and dependent variables was not caused by the control variable.

**BOX 10.2   What Can Happen When Controlling:
An Example**

A. All Cases (No Controls)

		INCOME	
		High	Low
VOTE	Republican	60%	40%
	Democrat	40	60
		100%	100%
		N = 500	500

Lambda = .20
Gamma = +.38
Phi² = .04
Chi² = 40.00
.001 > p

B. Relationship Unchanged: Controlling for Gender

MALES
INCOME

		High	Low
VOTE	Republican	60%	40%
	Democrat	40	60
		100%	100%
		N = 250	250

Lambda = .20
Gamma = +.38
Phi² = .04
Chi² = 20.00
.001 > p

FEMALES
INCOME

		High	Low
VOTE	Republican	60%	40%
	Democrat	40	60
		100%	100%
		N = 250	250

Lambda = .20
Gamma = +.38
Phi = .04
Chi² = 20.00
.001 > p

C. Relationship Weakened: Controlling for Ideology

LIBERALS
INCOME

		Low	High
VOTE	Republican	36%	36%
	Democrat	64	64
		100%	100%
		N = 55	420

Lambda = .00

CONSERVATIVES
INCOME

		Low	High
VOTE	Republican	63%	63%
	Democrat	37	37
		100%	100%
		N = 445	80

Lambda = .00

continues

continued

Gamma = .01	Gamma = .01
Phi^2 = .00	Phi^2 = .00
Chi^2 = .01	Chi^2 = .01
p > .90	p > .90

D. Relationship Strengthened: Controlling for Education

	COLLEGE INCOME			HIGH SCHOOL INCOME	
	High	Low		High	Low
VOTE Republican	58%	11%	VOTE Republican	86%	43%
Democrat	42	89	Democrat	14	89
	100%	100%		100%	100%
	N = 465	45		N = 35	455

Lambda = .18   Lambda = .08
Gamma = +.83   Gamma = +.78
Phi^2 = .07   Phi^2 = .05
Chi^2 = 36.54   Chi^2 = 24.55
.001 > p   .001 > p

E. Interaction: Controlling for Region

	NON-SOUTH INCOME			SOUTH INCOME	
	High	Low		High	Low
VOTE Republican	75%	17%	VOTE Republican	33%	75%
Democrat	25	83	Democrat	67	25
	100%	100%		100%	100%
	N = 320	300		N = 180	170

Lambda = .18   Lambda = .08
Lambda = .55   Lambda = .48
Gamma = +.88   Gamma = −.71
Phi^2 = .03   Phi^2 = .17
Chi^2 = 21.16   Chi^2 = 66.61
.001 > p   .001 > p

The second possibility is that the relationship is weakened, perhaps to the point of disappearing. This is shown in part C, where we control for ideology. A glance at the percentage tables shows that within the income categories there was no difference between the voting of high- and low-income individuals, and this is confirmed by all of the statistics. How is this possible? It came about because most of the high-income respondents were conservatives and most of the low-income respondents were liberals (as can be seen by the N's in the control tables). And since there was a strong tendency for conservatives to vote Republican and liberals to vote Democratic, income did not make any difference within those categories of ideology. When we have this sort of outcome, we conclude that the original relationship between the independent and dependent variable was caused by the control variable. If the relationship was weakened but did not disappear, we would say that it was partially caused by the control variable. In this example, where the original relationship completely disappeared, the control variable apparently was a complete cause of the relationship. In real-life situations it is rare that a relationship would disappear as completely as in this example, but significance tests like chi-square (assuming random sampling) tell us whether the relationship still exists or not.

There are two possible interpretations of this example. One is that the relationship is *spurious*—that the independent variable really does not affect the dependent. But it is also possible that the independent variable is an *intervening* factor between the other two variables. This is the more logical interpretation in this example. It would be reasonable to suppose that income affects a person's ideology and then ideology affects the voting decision. Determining which interpretation applies in a particular case involves the assumptions one makes about the *causal priority* of the variables. This reasoning is presented in detail later in this chapter.

A third possible outcome of controlling is that the original relationship is strengthened. This is illustrated by the example in part D of Box 10.2, where we control for education. As the percentage tables show, the contrast in voting between high- and low-income respondents is greater within the college and high school education categories than it was when all respondents were pooled in the original table, and this is confirmed by the higher value of the correlational statistics. This means that the effect of the control variable was to "hide" the relationship between the independent and dependent variable to some extent.

How can this happen? It occurs because the control variable has a relationship with the dependent variable *in the opposite direction* from that of the independent variable. In this example, respondents with college experience actually tend to vote more for Democrats. But there is a strong positive relationship between education and income; people who went to college tend to have higher incomes. Therefore, the effect of education was to reduce the apparent correlation between income and voting. This makes an important point: Even when there appears to be little or no relationship between the independent and dependent variables when looking at all the cases at once, it may be valuable to control for other factors.

The final possible outcome of controlling is that the relationship is different within the various categories of the control variable. Part E of Box 10.2 shows an example of this phenomenon, which is called *interaction*. When we control for region, we see that the relationship between income and vote becomes stronger for non-South respondents, but actually reverses direction for respondents who live in the South. Among these southerners, high income is associated with Democratic voting and low income with Republican voting. Interpreting interactive results is difficult, but it often suggests that we need to look more closely at other factors that might account for the difference between the categories of the control variable. In this example of income, voting, and region, we might need to look at variables such as the respondent's race and religion, because the North and South have different distributions on those characteristics. Although the example in part E would not be realistic today, it might have been found in earlier decades when there was a tendency for African Americans (most of whom were low-income southerners) to vote Republican, whereas high-income whites in the South typically supported a conservative Democratic party. Additional examples of controlling with contingency tables are found in Exercises A and B at the end of the chapter.

Given the range of effects third variables can have on relationships, it is extremely important to control for additional variables, particularly in the correlational design. Although controlling techniques are not an inherent part of the experimental and quasi-experimental designs, they can also be applied to the data resulting from those methods. How does one know which variables should be selected as controls? There is no simple answer, for the decision must be based on our theoretical understanding of the subject under study as well as on past research findings.

But it is important to remember one principle: *A control variable can affect a relationship only if it is related to both the independent and dependent variables.* For example, if there is no difference between geographic regions and the relative proportion of males and females (and therefore no correlation between region and gender), then there would be no purpose in using gender as a control variable when investigating the effect of region on anything else.

Our examples here have looked only at controlling for one variable at a time. But it is theoretically possible to control simultaneously for the effect of several variables using contingency tables. This is done by looking at the independent/dependent relationship within each possible combination of the categories on two or more control variables. Thus, the example in Box 10.2 might look like this:

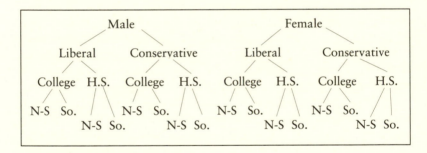

The result would be sixteen tables, each relating income and voting for one of the combinations of categories, such as male conservatives with a college education living in the South. Although this could easily be done, especially by a computer, the drawback is that each of the resulting tables would be based on relatively few cases, especially if some control variables had highly unequal category frequencies. Moreover, the control variables in the examples we have looked at thus far have been dichotomies, but it is common for control variables to have three or more categories. Therefore, unless one has an extremely large data set, controlling simultaneously for several variables requires another approach. The interval techniques described in the next section provide such an alternative.

Controlling with Interval Variables:
Partial Correlations

The procedure presented in Chapter 9 for regression and calculation of the Pearson correlation for interval variables can be extended in several ways to look at the relationships between three or more variables. The simplest technique, and the one most similar to the results of controlling with contingency tables, is *partial correlation*.

The partial correlation measures the relationship between an independent variable and a dependent variable when one or more other variables are controlled. The partial correlation coefficient is simply an extension of Pearson's r. It requires that the variables (three or more) be interval. It has the same range of −1 to +1 and the same interpretation, that is, the squared value is equal to the proportion of variance explained.

Subscripts are used to distinguish the different correlations involved. Although normally Pearson's correlation is referred to simply as r, it must now be designated with subscripts, for example, r_{yx}, meaning that it is the correlation between variable Y and variable X. Any convenient symbols, whether letters or numbers, may be used for this purpose. It is customary to list the dependent variable first.

Multivariate analyses often use a *correlation matrix*. This is a rectangular listing of a set of variables, so that the cell at which the row and column for two variables intersect reports the correlation coefficient for those variables. An example appears below.

	EDUCATION E	INCOME I	LIBERALISM L	VOTE V
Education (E)	1.00	.81	.43	−.23
Income (I)	.81	1.00	−.54	−.72
Liberalism (L)	.43	−.54	1.00	.41
Vote (V)	−.23	−.72	.41	1.00

$r_{ei} = .81$, $r_{le} = .43$, $r_{ve} = -.23$, $r_{li} = -.54$, $r_{vi} = -.72$, $r_{vl} = .41$

Note that the values along the diagonal are all 1.00. This is because they each represent the correlation of a variable with itself. Each of the other numbers appears twice because the correlation of variable X with variable Y is the same as the correlation of variable Y with variable X. Therefore, it is common to see correlation matrices presented as only one diagonal half. The line under the matrix shows the use of subscripts to report the same information. The correlation between education (E) and income (I) is written as r_{ei}, and the matrix shows it to be .81. The correlation between liberalism and education is r_{le} = .43.

With this notation system, it is relatively easy to compute a partial correlation from the "simple" Pearson correlations between variables. Here we will look only at the formula for the *first-order partial*, that is, *the correlation between the independent and dependent variables with only one control variable*. The formula is:

$$r_{yx.z} = \frac{r_{yx} - (r_{yz})(r_{xz})}{\sqrt{(1 - r_{yx}^2)(1 - r_{yz}^2)}}$$

where the subscript y denotes the dependent variables, x the independent variable, and z the control variable. As partial correlations can have any number of control variables, a period is used to separate them from the independent and dependent variables (e.g., $r_{yx.z}$).

The following example illustrates the computation of partial r. Suppose we took a random sample of 100 counties in the United States and found that the dependent variable, crime rate (C), and the independent variable, per capita income (I), had a correlation, r_{ci}, of .20, seemingly indicating that areas with higher-income residents had somewhat higher crime rates. However, we wish to control for percentage urban (U). To do this, we need to employ the correlations of both crime and income with percentage urban. Suppose these were r_{iu} = .60 and r_{cu} = .80. To compute the partial, we need to substitute these three simple correlations into the formula above, as follows:

$$r_{ci.u} = \frac{r_{ci} - (r_{cu})(r_{iu})}{\sqrt{(1 - r_{cu}^2)(1 - r_{iu}^2)}} = \frac{20 - (.80)(.60)}{\sqrt{(1 - (.80)^2)(1 - (.60)^2)}}$$

$$= \frac{.20 - .48}{\sqrt{(1 - .64)(1 - .36)}} = \frac{-.28}{\sqrt{(.36)(.64)}} = \frac{-.28}{.48} = -.58$$

The result shows that controlling for urbanization clearly had an effect on the relationship between income and crime. The original correlation was positive ($r_{ci} = .20$), but the partial, controlling for urbanization, was stronger and negative ($r_{ci.u} = -.58$). What occurred here? Although the initial relationship between crime and income level was surprisingly negative, we see that an even stronger correlate of crime was urbanization; the more urban an area, the higher the crime rate. And the more urban the county, the higher the income. When we control for urbanization, thereby removing its effects, we see that the real relationship between income and crime is negative, that is, the higher the income, the lower the crime rate.

Box 10.3 summarizes the critical information on partial r and gives another example of its computation. Additional examples can be found in Exercise C at the end of the chapter.

Significance Test for Partial r

Assuming that the data are from a random sample, the F-test can be used to determine significance in much the same way as with Pearson's r. There are two differences, however, both resulting from the fact that a partial correlation is based on more variables than a simple Pearson's r.

The formula for F is:

$$F = \frac{r_{xy.z}^2 (N - k - 1)}{1 - r_{xy.z}^2}$$

where N is the number of cases and k is the number of independent and control variables. This is actually the same formula as was used to calculate F for the simple Pearson's r, but since there was only one independent variable, the value of $(N - k - 1)$ was always $(N - 2)$. The formula above can be used for partials with any number of control variables.

Also different is that in this case we must use a probability of F table that takes into account the number of variables as well as the number of cases. This necessitates a different table for each level of probability. The table for the .05 level is reproduced in Table 10.1.

BOX 10.3   Information About Partial and
Multiple Correlations, the F-Test, and
Examples of Computations

Statistic: Partial r
Type: Measure of association
Assumption: Three or more interval variables
Range: −1 to +1
Interpretation: Proportion of variance explained ($r_{xy.z}{}^2$)
Formula:

$$r_{yx.z} = \frac{r_{yx} - (r_{yz})(r_{xz})}{\sqrt{(1 - r_{yz}^2)(1 - r_{xz}^2)}}$$

Example: Given the following correlation matrix of Pearson's r's, calculate the partial correlation between a respondent's reported Frequency of Voting (V) with Income (I), controlling for Years of Education (E), i.e., r_{ive}. Data are from a random sample of 500.

Matrix of Pearson's r

	I	E	V
Income (I)	1.00	.80	.50
Education (E)	.80	1.00	.60
Frequency of voting (V)	.50	.60	1.00

$$r_{vi.e}^2 = \frac{r_{vi} - (r_{ve})(r_{ie})}{\sqrt{(1 - r_{ve}^2)(1 - r_{ie}^2)}} = \frac{.50 - (.60)(.80)}{\sqrt{(1 - (.60)^2)(1 - (.80)^2)}}$$

$$= \frac{.50 - .48}{\sqrt{(1 - .36)(1 - .64)}} = \frac{.02}{\sqrt{.23}} \cdot \frac{.02}{.48} = .04$$

Conclusion: Although there was an initial fairly strong positive correlation between income and voting frequency, it almost completely disappeared when education was controlled for. This suggests that the tendency for respondents with higher education

continues

continued

to vote more frequently is almost entirely due to their higher level of education.

Statistic: F-test for partial R
Assumption: Random sampling
Interpretation: The probability of F is the probability that the partial correlation observed in the sample data could occur by chance if there were no relationship in the population from which the sample was drawn.
Formula:

$$F = \frac{r^2_{xy.z}(N - k - 1)}{1 - r^2_{xy.z}}$$

Example: Using the partial correlation computed above, $r_{vi.e}$ = .04, N = 500, and k = 2 (there are two independent variables). We substitute the values into the formula for F:

$$F = \frac{(.04)^2(500 - 2 - 1)}{1 - (.04)^2} = \frac{(.0017)(497)}{1 - .0017} = \frac{.84}{.998} = .85$$

Using Table 10.1, we locate the F value for N − k − 1 = 120 (the next-lowest to 497) and the column under the heading k = 2. The value there is 3.07, which is much larger than the F for this example. Therefore, the probability is greater than .05 and this partial correlation is not significant.

Statistic: Multiple R
Type: Measure of association
Assumption: Three or more interval variables
Range: 0 to +1
Interpretation: Proportion of variance explained (R^2)
Formula:

$$R^2_{y.xz} = \frac{r^2_{yx} + r^2_{yz} - 2(r_{yx})(r_{yz})(r_{xz})}{1 - r^2_{xz}}$$

continues

continued

Example: Using the correlation matrix in the first part of this table, we can calculate the multiple correlation of the independent variable, voting frequency (V) with two independent variables, income (I) and education (E). The Pearson's r correlations needed are rvi = .50, rve = .60, and r_{ie} = .80.

$$R^2_{v.ie} = \frac{r^2_{vu} + r^2_{ve} - 2(r_{vi})(r_{ve})(r_{ie})}{1 - r^2_{ie}}$$

$$= \frac{(.50)^2 + (.60)^2 - 2(.50)(.60)(.80)}{1-(.80)^2} = \frac{.25 + .36 - .48}{1 - .64}$$

$$= \frac{.13}{.36} = .36$$

Conclusion: Income and education together explain 36 percent of the variance in frequency of voting. This is virtually no improvement over the explanatory value of education alone.

Statistic: F-test for multiple R
Assumption: Random sampling
Interpretation: The probability of F is the probability that the partial correlation observed in the sample data could occur by chance if there were no relationship in the population from which the sample was drawn.

Formula:

$$F = \frac{R^2_{y.xz}(N - k - 1)}{(1 - R^2_{y.xz})(k)}$$

where N = sample size, and k = number of independent variables.

Example: To test the multiple R previously computed for voting frequency, income, and education, we substitute the relevant values: $r^2_{v.ie}$ = .36, N = 500, and k = 2.

continues

continued

$$F = \frac{(.36)(500 - 2 - 1)}{(1 - .36)(2)} = \frac{(.36)(497)}{(.64)(2)} = \frac{178.9}{1.28} = 139.8$$

We then go to Table 10.1. We look down to the line to N – k – 1 = 120 (the next-lowest value to 497) and to the column headed k = 2. The value there is 3.07. Since our F is much larger, we can conclude that the probability of chance occurrence is less than .05. Therefore, R^2 is significant.

To find the significance for the partial we just computed, we insert the values into the formula for F: N = 100, r = –.58, and k = 2. This results in the following:

$$F = \frac{(-.58)^2 (10 - 2 - 1)}{1 - (-.58)^2} = \frac{(.34)(97)}{1 - .34} = \frac{32.6}{.66} = 49.39$$

We now look in Table 10.1. We go down to the line opposite 60 (the closest one to the value of 97 for N – k – 1) and look at the second column, because k, the number of independent and control variables is 2. We see that an F value of only 3.15 would be required to assure that the probability of chance occurrence of this relationship would be less than .05. Since our F is much larger, we are sure that the relationship is significant at the .05 level. Other examples of the F-test for the partial correlation can be found in Box 10.3 and in the Exercises at the end of the chapter.

The Multiple Correlation

Dependent variables in social research commonly have several distinct but related causes. Consider, for example, an individual's vote for a presidential candidate. This decision can be partially predicted or explained by each of a considerable number of factors, including the person's party identification, income, race, religion, ideology, and attitudes toward a number of specific issues. But these factors are themselves interrelated; for example, a Republican identifier will tend to have a higher income and a more conservative ideology. Simply adding up the explanatory value of these separate independent

174

TABLE 10.1   Probability of F for Partial and Multiple Correlations
(0.5 Probability Level)

k = Number of independent and control variables						
N–k–1	k = 1	k = 2	k = 3	k = 4	k = 5	k = 6
1	161.4	199.5	215.7	224.6	230.2	234.0
2	18.51	19.00	19.16	19.25	19.30	19.33
3	10.13	9.55	9.28	9.12	9.01	8.94
4	7.71	6.94	6.59	6.39	6.26	6.16
5	6.61	5.79	5.41	5.19	5.05	4.95
6	5.99	5.14	4.76	4.53	4.39	4.28
7	5.59	4.74	4.35	4.12	3.97	3.87
8	5.32	4.46	4.07	3.84	3.69	3.58
9	5.12	4.26	3.86	3.63	3.48	3.37
10	4.96	4.10	3.71	3.48	3.33	3.22
11	4.84	3.98	3.59	3.36	3.20	3.09
12	4.75	3.88	3.49	3.26	3.11	3.00
13	4.67	3.80	3.41	3.18	3.02	2.92
14	4.60	3.74	3.34	3.11	2.96	2.85
15	4.54	3.68	3.29	3.06	2.90	2.79
16	4.49	3.63	3.24	3.01	2.85	2.74
17	4.45	3.59	3.20	2.96	2.81	2.70
18	4.41	3.55	3.16	2.93	2.77	2.66
19	4.38	3.52	3.13	2.90	2.74	2.63
20	4.35	3.49	3.10	2.87	2.71	2.60
21	4.32	3.47	3.07	2.84	2.68	2.57
22	4.30	3.44	3.05	2.82	2.66	2.55
23	4.28	3.42	3.03	2.80	2.64	2.53
24	4.26	3.40	3.01	2.78	2.62	2.51
25	4.24	3.38	2.99	2.76	2.60	2.49
26	4.22	3.37	2.89	2.74	2.59	2.47
27	4.21	3.35	2.96	2.73	2.57	2.46
28	4.20	3.34	2.95	2.71	2.56	2.44
29	4.18	3.33	2.93	2.70	2.54	2.43
30	4.17	3.32	2.92	2.69	2.53	2.42

continues

continued						
40	4.08	3.23	2.84	2.61	2.45	2.34
60	4.00	3.15	2.76	2.52	2.37	2.25
120	3.92	3.07	2.68	2.45	2.29	2.17
Infinity	3.84	2.99	2.60	2.37	2.21	2.09

NOTE: Larger tables showing additional significance levels may be found in many comprehensive statistics texts.

SOURCE: Ronald A. Fisher and Frank Yates, *Statistical Tables for Biological, Agricultural, and Medical Research, Sixth Edition* (Edinburgh: Oliver and Boyd, 1963), pp 53, 55, 57.

© R. A. Fisher and F. Yates. Reprinted by permission of Pearson Education, Limited.

variables would be misleading, for their contributions to the vote, in effect, "overlap" to some degree. The multiple correlation coefficient is designed to measure the total contribution of several independent variables to the explanation of a single dependent variable while taking into account any "overlap" in their contribution.

The multiple correlation coefficient is symbolized by a capital R, and the subscripts begin with the dependent variable, followed by the independent variables. Thus $R_{y.xz}$ measures the total effect of the independent variables, x and z, on y, the dependent variable. The details of multiple R are similar to those Pearson's r and the partial r in that *all variables must be interval* and that *the squared value of R is the equal to proportion of variance explained.* However, multiple R differs from the others in that it can *only be positive,* that is, it does not show direction (because some of the independent variables may have a positive relationship to the dependent variable and others a negative relationship). Therefore, the range of possible values for R is 0 to +1.

As with the partial correlation, multiple R can easily be calculated from the simple Pearson's r values. Normally the square of multiple R is computed, which tells us the proportion of variance explained; thus, for multiple R^2 with two independent variables, the formula is:

$$R^2_{y.xz} = \frac{r^2_{yx} + r^2_{yz} - 2(r_{yx})(r_{yz})(r_{xz})}{1 - r^2_{xz}}$$

R itself can be calculated by taking the square root of the result, but R^2 is more meaningful and hence is the figure usually reported.

We can illustrate this computation with the previous example for crime rate (C), percent urban (U) and per capita income (I). The Pearson correlations were $r_{ic} = .20$, $r_{iu} = .60$, and $r_{cu} = .80$. Suppose we wish to compute the multiple correlation of two independent variables (income and percentage urban) with the dependent variable (crime rate). Substituting the letter identifying the variables for the example in the formula and then substituting the corresponding values, we have:

$$R^2_{c.iu} = \frac{r^2_{ci} + r^2_{cu} - 2(r_{ci})(r_{cu})(r_{iu})}{1 - r^3_{iu}}$$

$$= \frac{(.20)^2 + (.80)^2 - 2(.20)(80)(.60)}{1 - (.60)^2} = \frac{.04 + .64 - .19}{1 - .36} = \frac{.49}{.64} = .77$$

This shows that income and urbanization together explain 77 percent of the variance in crime rate.

Multiple correlations with more independent variables may be computed using more complicated formulas involving partial correlations.

Significance Test for R^2

Assuming that the data are from a random sample, the significance of R^2 may be determined by the F-test in much the same way as for the partial correlation. The formula is:

$$F = \frac{R^2_{y.xz}(N - k - 1)}{(1 - R^2_{y.xz})(k)}$$

where N is the sample size and k is the number of independent variables. For the preceding example, in which $R^2 = .77$, N = 100, and k = 2, we substitute these values and obtain:

$$F = \frac{.77 - (100 - 2 - 1)}{(1 - .77)(2)} = \frac{.77(97)}{(.23)(2)} = 162.36$$

(Note that the value of .77 previously computed for R^2 was already the squared value.)

Turning now to the probability figures in Table 10.1, we go down column 1 to where $N - k - 1$ is 60 (the table's next lowest value from 97) and then over to column 3 (headed "k = 2"). We see that in order to be statistically significant, F would have to equal 3.15 or more. Since our F is much larger, we can be confident that the probability of having obtained an R^2 value of .77 by chance is less than .05, and therefore the relationship is significant. Additional examples of the F-test for R^2 are found in Box 10.3 and in Exercise C at the end of the chapter.

Beta Weights

The process of determining the "best-fitting" regression line and the equation that defines it can be extended to any number of independent variables. The equation takes the form:

$$Y = a + b_1X_1 + b_2X_2 + b_3X_3 \dots b_nX_n$$

where Y is the dependent variable, X_1, X_2, and so on are the independent variables, and b_1, b_2, and so on are the corresponding values of the slope for each independent variable. The computations for these multiple regression statistics are beyond the scope of this book, and in fact they are almost always done on a computer. However, it is important to be aware of them as they are widely used in contemporary political science research.

Although the b values for the slopes are quite meaningful, they can be difficult to interpret directly because they are dependent on the units in which each of the variables is measured. For that reason, the results of multiple regression analyses are commonly reported in terms of *standardized regression coefficients* or *beta (β) weights*. Betas are standardized in two ways. First, they show the effect of each independent variable on the dependent variable, controlling for all of the other independent variables. In this respect, they are like partial correlations. Second, they use the standard deviations of the variables to remove the effects of the particular units in which the variables are measured. Thus if the beta for the first independent variable is twice as high as that for the second independent variable, we can say that the first variable had twice as much impact on the dependent variable as did the second. F-tests are used with betas to determine the significance of each independent variable. The multiple R^2 is a measure of the explanatory value of the whole equation.

Causal Interpretation

The chapter thus far has presented techniques for analyzing the relationship of three or more variables, particularly procedures for looking at the relationship between two variables while controlling for a third. This concluding section will focus on some principles that are vital for interpreting what the results of these techniques mean.

Criteria for Inferring Causality

Interpreting the results of multivariate analysis is a process leading to conclusions about *patterns of causation*. A quick review of the three "criteria for inferring causality" that were introduced in Chapter 3 will be useful here. The first is *covariation*, or correlation. You should now have a much clearer idea of what this means. The various measures of association, from lambda to multiple R, are all measures of covariation. The second criterion is *time order* or, more precisely, causal priority. To interpret the results of multivariate analysis correctly, we must be very clear about our assumptions about the order in which we believe the variables occur. Finally, before we can draw any causal inferences, we must make sure that relationships between variables are *not spurious*. This is the purpose of the controlling techniques discussed earlier in this chapter.

Causal Models

Although the process of causal modeling in its complete form is mathematically sophisticated and beyond the scope of this book, its essentials can be simplified and used to analyze a small number of variables with the techniques covered earlier. The key point is that we must be prepared to assume that *any causal relationship between two variables can be in only one direction*. It is quite possible for causation to be *reciprocal*, that is, for X to influence Y while Y influences X. For example, a person's ideology undoubtedly influences his or her party identification, but party loyalty may also affect ideological views. There are a number of techniques for analyzing two-way causation, but they require much more statistical background than can be provided here. Therefore, we must assume that causation is unidirectional and that we know what the direction is. When our data are derived from a true experiment or a quasi-experimental design, there is little doubt about which variable "came first" because we know when the variables occurred. However, with a correlational design (which is where we typically use causal modeling), this causal order is less clear. In that case the assumption of causal order must be based on the kind of reasoning presented in Chapter 2 in the discussion of the variables' theoretical role and the difference between independent and dependent variables. We must also make the assumption that there are no additional variables that could be affecting the relationships. But whatever the basis for the assumptions, we must specify the causal priority *before assessing* the applicability of any causal models.

Figure 10.1 illustrates the need for causal modeling in even the simplest case, where there are only three variables. We first specify the causal priority X, Y, Z. This means that if there is causation between the three variables, then X causes Y and Z, and Y causes Z. No reverse causation is permitted—that is, Y cannot cause X, and Z cannot cause either of the other two.

We would undertake causal modeling for this set of variables because we have data that indicate some relationship between them; some or all of the possible intercorrelations are not zero. The example in Figure 10.1 assumes that we have interval data so that Pearson's r and partial r can be computed. But the same reasoning can be applied to nominal and ordinal data, as will be discussed later.

As Figure 10.1 shows, there are four possible causal models that might underlie a pattern of observed intercorrelation between only three variables. We can use Pearson's r and partial correlations to determine whether each model fits any given set of data. Model 1 is the simplest case, where there are two independent variables, X and Y, that are not at all related. We would conclude that this is the case only if there were no simple Pearson correlation between X and Y, that is, $r_{YX} = 0$.

FIGURE 10.1   Causal models for three variables and tests

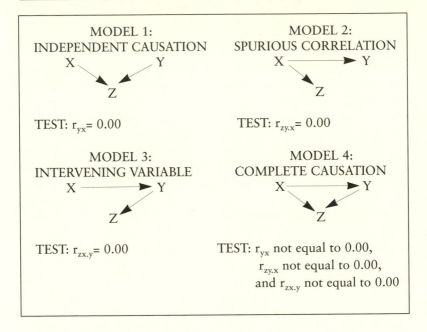

Model 2 in Figure 10.1 illustrates *spurious correlation*, in which there is some apparent relationship between two variables (Y and Z in this case), but that relationship disappears when controlled for a prior variable (X in this case). The test for this model is the partial correlation between Z and Y, controlling for X. If $r_{yz.x} = 0$, then we would conclude that model 2 fits our data.

Model 3 illustrates the presence of an *intervening variable*, that is, X causes Y, and then Y causes Z. This means that while we may have observed some correlation between X and Z, it occurs only through Y, the intervening variable. Therefore, the test for this model is the partial correlation between Z and X, controlling for Y. If $r_{zx.y} = 0$, then we can conclude that model 3 can be applied to this data set.

The difference between model 2 and model 3 highlights the importance of the assumptions we make about causal priority. If we find that a correlation between two variables disappears when we control for a third, does that mean that the original relationship was spurious? No, not unless the control variable was logically prior to the independent variable. If the control variable was more likely a result of the independent variable, then the model 3 interpretation of an intervening factor is correct. If, on the other hand, we have assumed that the control variable is causally prior to the other two, then their relationship would be spurious.

If none of the test correlations (r_{yx}, $r_{yz.x}$, and $r_{zx.y}$) are equal to zero, then model 4 applies. This means that, given our assumptions and available information, we cannot simplify the model and must assume that all of the correlations do imply causal linkages. It is also possible that more than one of these test statistics will be equal to zero. This simply means that some or all of these variables are not even related, so there is no need for causal interpretation. However, one should not draw such a conclusion until the appropriate partials have been computed, because it is possible for the value of Pearson's r between two variables to be zero while the partial is significantly positive or negative.

Although examples such as these—in which correlations turn out to be exactly zero—can occur with real data, usually they do not. How close to zero must a correlation be? If the data are from a random sample, then the F-test may be used for Pearson's r and the partial correlations. If the probability is greater than .05, then the correlation can be assumed to be zero for the population. But one may be working with nonsample data, where any correlation, however small, is, in a statistical sense, significant, or with data from a such large sample that even minute correlations indicating no practical relationship are still significant at the .05 level. In such instances, one may look at all of the tests and see that because one of the test statistics is extremely weak, the corresponding model is, indeed, the "best fitting."

Box 10.4 illustrates the process of causal modeling with an example using data on nations. The dependent variable is military spending (measured as a percentage of national budget). The causal priority of the other two variables is not obvious, as both wealth (measured as per capita GNP) and democracy (measured on a ten-point scale) would have a lengthy history. To keep the example simple, we will assume that wealth causes democracy. Hence the causal priority is wealth, democracy, military spending. As Box 10.4 shows, model 1, independent causation, clearly does not apply, because wealth and democracy are strongly correlated. Model 2, spurious correlation, also does not apply, because the partial r between military spending and wealth, controlling for democracy ($r_{mw.d}$), is quite strong. But when we test model 3, Intervening Variable, we find that the partial correlation between military spending and wealth, controlling for democracy, is very nearly zero ($r_{md.w} = .05$). Hence we conclude that model 2 is the best fit. The wealthier a nation, the more democratic it tends to be, and the more democratic, the higher the military spending. In other words, the apparent relationship of wealth to military spending is a result of the effect of wealth on the type of government. Another example of causal modeling can be found in Exercise C at the end of the chapter.

The relatively simple three-variable example in Box 10.4 illustrates how controlling allows us to understand these basic patterns in statistical analysis, particularly to distinguish cases of intervening variables from spurious correlations. More elaborate models may be constructed for larger numbers of variables. Although that is best done by writing simultaneous equations for all of the possible patterns (Blalock 1964), the relatively simple approach using partial correlations can easily be extended to more complex problems (Blalock 1962).

Figure 10.2 shows a causal model that Schulman and Pomper (1975) constructed to analyze voting behavior in the 1972 presidential election. As is common in the presentation of such models, measures of the relative strength (in this case, beta weights) are included for each of the causal arrows. This model shows how the effects of social background and family partisanship are mediated largely through an individual's party identification. Party identification then has both a direct effect on the vote and an indirect effect through its influence on attitudes toward particular issues and evaluation of the candidates. Interestingly, almost identical causal patterns were found for elections in three different decades, but the relative strength of the different linkages showed that party identification declined somewhat as an influence on voting while the importance of issues increased. Thus, causal modeling can reveal important generalizations about complex phenomena.

Causal Interpretation Using Contingency Tables

Although the complete causal modeling procedure requires interval data and partial correlations, the same logic can be applied to nominal and ordinal category data, in which controlling is done using contingency tables as explained in the first part of this chapter. To do this for three variables, explicit assumptions must be made about causal priorities. Then three sets of contingency tables must

BOX 10.4   An Example of Causal Modeling

Correlation Matrix (Pearson's r)

	W	D	M
Wealth (W)	1.00	.85	.51
Democracy (D)	.85	1.00	.62
Military spending (M)	.51	.62	1.00

Relevant Partials:
$r_{md.w} = .78$
$r_{mw.d} = -.05$

N = 180 Nations

Assumed causal priority: Wealth, democracy, military spending

Model 1: Independent Causation

Test: Does $r_{dw} = 0$? No, $r_{dw} = .85$
Conclusion: Model 1 does not apply.

Model 2: Spurious Correlation

Test: Does $r_{md.w} = 0$? No, $r_{md.w} = .78$.
Conclusion: Model 2 does not apply.

Model 3: Intervening Variable

Test: Does $r_{mw.d} = 0$? $r_{md.w} = -.05$,
which is very close to zero.
Conclusion: Model 3 may apply.

Model 4: Complete Causation

Test: Are r_{dw}, $r_{md.w}$, and $r_{mw.d}$ all not
equal to zero? Since $r_{md.w} = .05$,
Model 4 does not apply very well.

continues

continued

Conclusion: Model 3 is the best fitting causal model:

be constructed: (1) tables cross-tabulating each pair of variables without controls; (2) tables cross-tabulating the second independent ("middle") variable with the dependent variable while controlling for the first independent variable; and (3) tables cross-tabulating the first independent variable with the dependent variable while controlling for the second independent ("middle") variable. Appropriate statistical measures of association and (if random sample data are used) significance levels are then computed. When all of this has been done, it may be possible to distinguish the four possible causal models previously presented.

The results of this procedure may be more ambiguous than those obtained in causal modeling for interval variables. The problem is that there may be substantial *interaction*, that is, the relationship may be of different strengths within different categories of a control variable. On the other hand, this can be an advantage of the contingency table method, since partial correlations do not reveal whether interaction is present. The contingency table approach also may be extended to a larger number of variables, which would require controlling for two or more variables at once. As noted earlier, simultaneously controlling for several variables produces numerous tables, many with inadequate numbers of cases.

Box 10.5 presents the contingency tables necessary to undertake this version of causal analysis. The example deals with the question of racial differences in voting participation and the extent to which these differences can be attributed to education. We assume that the causal priority is race, education, turnout. That turnout could only be a consequence of the other two is obvious. It also makes sense to assume that race more likely influences education (i.e., members of minority groups tend to have less education) for a variety of reasons, whereas the notion that education could influence race and ethnicity does not make sense.

FIGURE 10.2   An example of a causal model: 1972 presidential election

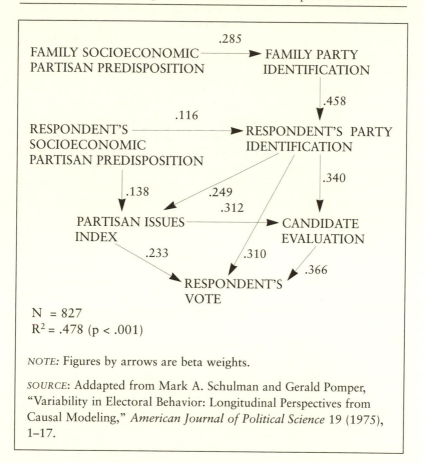

N = 827
R² = .478 (p < .001)

NOTE: Figures by arrows are beta weights.

SOURCE: Addapted from Mark A. Schulman and Gerald Pomper,
"Variability in Electoral Behavior: Longitudinal Perspectives from
Causal Modeling," *American Journal of Political Science* 19 (1975),
1–17.

Box 10.5 first presents the relationships between each pair of
variables. It then explores the relationship between the dependent
variable (turnout) and each of the independent variables (race and
education). Recalling the four causal models presented earlier, we
can easily see that model 1, independent causation, is not a possibility, because the two independent variables (race and education)
are strongly related. The second set of tables (turnout with education, controlling for race) would test model 2, spurious correlation,
because it determines whether the relationship between the second
and third variables disappears when controlling for the first. Model

2 does not fit the data, as the turnout/education relationship remains about the same strength and is significant for both racial categories. But when we look at the relationship between turnout and race, controlling for education, the relationship within each education category virtually disappears, in both strength and significance. When we compare individuals of a given level of education, there is virtually no difference in the turnout rates of whites and nonwhites. Since we have assumed that race is causally prior to education, model 3, intervening variable, fits these data very well. This analysis aids in our substantive interpretation of turnout. Race is not irrelevant to turnout, because it is ultimately a cause, but it had its entire effect through education. This might suggest that if we are concerned about increasing turnout among racial minorities, we should address the larger question of why there are racial differences in educational attainment.

Exercises

Answers to the exercises follow. It is recommended that you attempt to complete the exercises before looking at the answers.

Exercise A

Below are tables showing the relationship between party competition and spending for education in the fifty states with a control for the state's per capita income. What conclusion would you draw about the hypothesis that higher levels of party competition cause states to spend more on education?

CONTROLLING FOR INCOME								
(ALL CASES) COMPETITION			HIGH INCOME COMPETITION			LOW INCOME COMPETITION		
SPENDING	*High*	*Low*	SPENDING	*High*	*Low*	SPENDING	*High*	*Low*
High	72%	36%		85%	83%		20%	21%
Low	28	64		15	17		80	79
	100%	100%		100%	100%		100%	100%
	N = 25	25		N = 20	6		N= 5	19
	Gamma = +.64			Gamma = +.06			Gamma = −.03	

BOX 10.5   Using Contingency Tables for Causal Interpretation

Assumed causal priority: Race, education, turnout

A. Tables with No Controls

	RACE	
TURNOUT	*White*	*Non-white*
Voter	70%	50%
Non-voter	30	50
	100%	100%
	N = 1,000	400

Gamma = .40
  Chi^2 = 49.51 (p < .001)
  Phi^2 = .04

	RACE	
EDUCATION	*White*	*Non-white*
College	60%	25%
High School	40	75
	100%	100%
	N = 1,000	400

Gamma = .63
  Chi^2 = 140.00 (p < .001)
  Phi^2 = .10

	EDUCATION	
TURNOUT	*College*	*High School*
Voter	71%	29%
Non-voter	29	71
	100%	100%
	N = 700	700

Gamma = .72
Chi^2 = 257.14 (p < .001)
Phi^2 = .18

B. Turnout by Education, Controlling for Race

	WHITES EDUCATION	
TURNOUT	*College*	*High School*
Voter	72%	30%
Non-voter	28	70
	100%	100%
	N = 600	400

Gamma = .71
  Chi^2 = 168.35 (p < .001)
  Phi^2 = .17

	NON-WHITES EDUCATION	
TURNOUT	*College*	*High School*
Voter	70%	30%
Non-voter	30	70
	100%	100%
	N = 100	300

Gamma = .68
  Chi^2 = 50.00 (p < .001)
  Phi^2 = .12

continues

continued

C. Turnout by Race, Controlling for Education

	COLLEGE			**HIGH SCHOOL**	
	RACE			**RACE**	
TURNOUT	*White*	*Non-white*	TURNOUT	*White*	*Non-white*
Voter	72%	70%	*Voter*	30%	30%
Non-voter	28	30	*Non-voter*	70	70
	100%	100%		100%	100%
	N = 600	100		N = 400	300

Gamma = .04   Gamma = .00
  Chi² = 0.57 (p > .80)   Chi² = 0.00 (p > .99)
  Phi² = .00   Phi² = .00

The best-fitting model would look like this:
Race ———▶ Education
Turnout

Exercise B

Below are tables showing the relationship between a respondent's approval rating of the president and his or her vote in the next election with a control for the respondent's party identification. What conclusion would you draw about the hypothesis that people who approve of the president's performance in office are more likely to vote for the candidate of the president's party? (As you might guess, the president in this example was a Democrat.) Data are from a survey using random sampling.

(ALL CASES)	CONTROLLING FOR PARTY IDENTIFICTION				
				DEMOCRATS	
	APPROVAL			**APPROVAL**	
VOTE	*Approve*	*Disapprove*	VOTE	*Approve*	*Disapprove*
Demo.	80%	20%		90%	50%
Repub.	20	80		10	50
	100%	100%		100%	100%

continues

continued

N = 500	500	N = 200	100

Lambda = .60
Gamma = +.88
Chi ^{2} = 680.00 (p < .001)
Phi ^{2} = .68

Lambda = .69
Gamma = +.80
Chi ^{2} = 61.43 (p < .001)
Phi ^{2} = .20

CONTROLLING FOR
PARTY IDENTIFICATION

	REPUBLICANS APPROVAL			INDEPENDENTS APPROVAL	
VOTE	Approve	Disapprove		Approve	Disapprove
Demo.	60%	10%	VOTE	80%	15%
Repub.	40	90		20	85
	100%	100%		100%	100%
	N = 100	200		N = 200	200

Lambda = .25
Gamma = +.86
Chi ^{2} = 83.21 (p < .001)
Phi ^{2} = .28

Lambda = .63
Gamma = +.86
Chi ^{2} = 169.42 (p < .001)
Phi ^{2} = .42

Exercise C

Below is a matrix of Pearson's r data on a random sample of fifty nations that were all at some time in the past under the control of a colonial power. The variables are the number of years since independence, economic development (measured as per capita GDP), and political instability (measured as the relative number of "irregular executive transfers" that have occurred in the nation. Using the correlations in the matrix:

1. Calculate the partial correlation between instability and development, controlling for years since independence ($r_{id.y}$). Use the F-test to determine significance.
2. Calculate the partial correlation between instability and years since independence, controlling for development ($r_{iy.d}$). Use the F-test to determine significance.

3. Calculate the multiple correlation with instability as the dependent variable with development and years since independence as the independent variables. Use the F-test to determine significance.
4. Assuming the causal priority years since independence, development, instability, determine the best-fitting causal model for these variables.

	YEARS Y	DEVELOPMENT D	INSTABILITY I
Years (Y)	1.00	.34	−.52
Development (D)	.34	1.00	−.75
Instability (I)	−.52	−.75	1.00

Suggested Answers to Exercises

Exercise A

When we look at all the states, there appears to be a fairly strong positive relationship between party competition and spending on education, that is, states with high competition are more likely to be states with high spending than states with low competition. However, when we control for states' per capita income, the relationship almost completely disappears. This indicates that the relationship between competition and spending was due to the effect of income and that these two variables do not affect each other.

Exercise B

When we look at all respondents, we see that there is a strong and significant relationship between approval and the vote, that is, those who approved of presidential performance voted Democratic, and those who disapproved voted Republican. When we control for the respondent's party identification, the relationship remains strong and significant within each group of party identifiers. Therefore, we can conclude that presidential approval does affect voting in the next election. Note that (as you can tell from the N's in the control tables) party is related to both variables. Democratic identifiers are more likely to approve of presidential performance and are more likely to vote for the Democratic candidate. But the effect of approval is clear even within the party identification categories.

Exercise C

1.

$$r_{id.y} = \frac{r_{id} - (r_{iy})(r_{dy})}{\sqrt{(1 - r_{iy}^2)(1 - r_{dy}^2)}} = \frac{-.75 - (.34)(-.52)}{\sqrt{(1 - (.34)^2(1 - (-.52))}}$$

$$= \frac{-.75 + .18}{\sqrt{(1 - .12)(1 - .27)}} = \frac{-.57}{\sqrt{.64}} = \frac{-.57}{.80} = -.71$$

$$F = \frac{r_{id.y}^2 (N - k - 1)}{1 - r_{id.y}^2} = \frac{(-.71)^2 (50 - 2 - 1)}{1 - (-.71)^2} = \frac{(.50)(47)}{1 - .50}$$

$$= \frac{23.5}{.50} = 47.00$$

F > 3.21, so p < .05. This partial is significant.

2.

$$r_{iy.d} = \frac{r_{iy} - (r_{id})(r_{yd})}{\sqrt{(1 - r_{id}^2)(1 - r_{yd}^2)}} = \frac{-.52 - (.75)(-.34)}{\sqrt{(1 - (-.75)^2(1 - (-.34)^2)}}$$

$$\frac{-.52 + .26}{\sqrt{(1 - .56)(1 - .12)}} = \frac{-.26}{\sqrt{(.44)(.88)}} = \frac{-.26}{\sqrt{.38}}$$

$$r_{iy.d}^2 = \frac{-.26}{.62} = -.42$$

$$F = \frac{r_{iy.d}^2 (N - k - 1)}{1 - r_{iy.d}^2} = \frac{(-.42)^2 (50 - 2 - 1)}{1 - (-.42)^2} = \frac{(.18)(47)}{1 - .18}$$

$$= \frac{8.29}{.82} = 10.06$$

F > 3.21, so p < .05. This partial is significant.

3.

$$R_{iy.d}^2 = \frac{r_{id}^2 + r_{iy}^2 - 2(r_{id})(r_{iy})(r_{dy})}{1 - r_{dy}^2}$$

$$= \frac{(-.75)^2 + (-.52)^2 - 2(-.75)(-.52)(.34)}{1 - (.34)^2}$$

$$= \frac{.56 + .27 - .27}{1 - .12}$$

$$R_{iy.d}^2 = \frac{-.56}{.88} = .64$$

$$F = \frac{r_{i.dy}^2(N - k - 1)}{(1 - R_{id.y}^2)(k)} = \frac{.64(50 - 2 - 1)}{(1 - .64)(2)} = \frac{.64(47)}{(.36)(2)}$$

$$= \frac{30.08}{.72} = 41.77$$

F > 3.23, so p < .05. R is significant.

4.

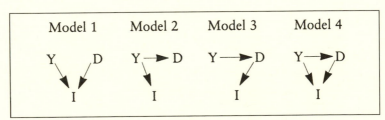

The test for model 1, independent causation, is whether the simple Pearson correlation between years since independence and development is zero. As the matrix shows, $r_{dy} = .34$ (and an F-test shows that this is significant at the .05 level). Therefore, model 1 does not apply.

The test for model 2, spurious correlation, is whether the partial correlation between instability and development, controlling for years since independence, is zero. As the calculations in question 1 above show, $r_{id.y} = -.71$ and it is significant. Therefore, model 2 does not apply.

The test for model 3, intervening variable, is whether the partial correlation between instability and years since independence, controlling for development, is zero. As the calculations in question 2 above show, $r_{iy.d} = -.42$ and it is significant. Therefore, model 3 does not apply.

Since the data fail to meet any of the tests for the first three models, we conclude that model 4, complete causation, is the most applicable. Both years since independence and economic development (which are themselves interrelated) have a direct effect on political instability.

References

Almer, Ennis C. 2000. Statistical Tricks and Traps. Los Angeles: Pyrczak Publishing.

Ansolabehere, Stephen, et al. 1994. "Does Attack Advertising Demobilize the Electorate?" American Political Science Review 88: 829–838.

Berelson, Bernard. 1971. Content Analysis in Communication Research. New York: Hafner.

Blalock, Hubert M. 1962. "Four-Variable Causal Models and Partial Correlations," American Journal of Sociology 68: 182–194, 510–512.

———. 1964. Causal Inferences in Nonexperimental Research. Chapel Hill: University of North Carolina Press.

Cutright, Phillips. 1963. "Measuring the Impact of Local Party Activity on the General Election Vote," Public Opinion Quarterly 27: 372–386.

Edwards, George C. 1983. The Public Presidency. New York: St. Martin's.

Graber, Doris A. 1988. Processing the News, 2d ed. New York: Longman.

Huff, Darrell. 1954. How to Lie with Statistics. New York: W. W. Norton.

Katz, Daniel, and Samuel J. Eldersveld, "The Impact of Party Activity on the Electorate," Public Opinion Quarterly 25: 1–24.

Kramer, Gerald H. 1970. "The Impact of Party Activity on the Electorate," Public Opinion Quarterly 34: 560–572.

Monroe, Alan D. 1977. "Urbanism and Voter Turnout: A Note on Some Unexpected Findings," American Journal of Political Science 21: 71–81.

———. 1998. "Public Opinion and Public Policy, 1980–1993," Public Opinion Quarterly, 62: 6–28.

Mueller, John E. 1973. *War, Presidents, and Public Opinion.* New York: Wiley.

North, Robert C., et al., 1963. Content Analysis: A Handbook with Applications for the Study of International Crisis. Evanston, IL: Northwestern University Press.

Page, Benjamin I., and Robert Shapiro. 1983. "Effects of Public Opinion on Policy," American Political Science Review 77: 1071–1089.

Patterson, Thomas E. 1980. The Mass Media Election. New York: Praeger.

Pomper, Gerald M., with Susan S. Lederman. 1980. Elections in America, 2d ed. New York: Longman.

Robinson, Michael J., and Margaret A. Sheehan. 1983. Over the Wire and on TV. New York: Russell Sage.

Schulman, Mark A., and Gerald M. Pomper. 1975. "Variability in Electoral Behavior: Longitudinal Perspectives from Causal Modeling," American Journal of Political Science 21: 1–18.

Scott, Gregory M., and Stephen M. Garrison. 1998. The Student Political Science Writer's Manual, 2d ed. Upper Saddle River, NJ: Prentice Hall.

Tufte, Edward R. 1983. The Visual Display of Quantitative Information. Cheshire, CT: Graphics Press.

Wallgren, Anders, et al. 1996. Graphing Statistics and Data: Creating Better Charts. Thousand Oaks, CA: Sage Publications.

Wolfinger, Raymond E., and Steven J. Rosenstone. 1980. Who Votes? New Haven: Yale University Press.

Index